small town dreamer

★

FINDING COURAGE TO
CHASE YOUR BIGGEST DREAMS
IN RURAL AMERICA

DANNA LARSON

FOUNDER OF RURAL REVIVAL

Small Town Dreamer
Finding Courage to Chase Your Biggest Dreams in Rural America

www.smalltowndreamer.co
www.ruralrevival.co

For speaking inquiries, please complete the form at ruralrevival.co/contact.

Cover and interior designed by Branded by Rural Revival.

ISBN 979-8-9931255-0-3 (paperback)
ISBN 979-8-9931255-1-0 (ebook)
ISBN 979-8-9931255-2-7 (audiobook)

DEDICATION

To the small-town dreamers—the steadfast believers, tireless builders, and unsung heroes who anchor your communities with hope.

To every heart that's faced giants in solitude, wrestled fears in prayer, and longed for the blueprint of your calling to unfold in your rural corner of the world.

This is for you.

May your vision be awakened. May your dreams take flight. May your hope be renewed. And may your legacy shine brightly.

Rural America needs you now, more than ever, to carry the torch of possibility.

FROM THE AUTHOR

You might know me as the voice behind the *Rural Revival* podcast, where I've become an unexpected cheerleader for the dreamers of rural America. When I launched the podcast seven years ago, my goal was simple: shine a light on the incredible people doing extraordinary things in small towns. I hoped their stories would spark a fire, inspiring others to dream big right where they are. And guess what? It's happening!

Through *Rural Revival*, I've had the privilege of meeting so many of you—the most inspiring people breathing life into your communities and chasing dreams I could hardly imagine. Our conversations have fueled my own hopes for what's possible, not just for our towns but for ourselves. I've dreamed alongside you, and it's changed me. It even led me back to my own hometown, where I've discovered something unexpected. This journey isn't just about saving our towns; it's about reviving *us*. And as we dare to live out our dreams, we pave the way for others to do the same.

Something is stirring in rural America—a new era is dawning. Can you feel it? The ground is shifting, and an extraordinary opportunity lies before us. Let's not miss it.

As it turns out, rural America is a place where we can grow roots and spread our wings. It's brimming with possibility. We no longer have to leave our small towns to chase our dreams because this is a place where dreams are waiting to happen.

In the pages ahead, my hope is to stir those dreams buried in your heart, to call them forth, and to cheer you on as you bring them to life. This is your invitation to step into *more*—because it's time.

Danna Larson
Rural Revival Founder and Small Town Dreamer

CONTENTS

CHAPTER ONE
YOUR FIELD OF DREAMS   13

CHAPTER TWO
ROOTS & WINGS   25

CHAPTER THREE
DARE TO DREAM AGAIN   39

CHAPTER FOUR
IT'S NOT JUST ABOUT YOU   55

CHAPTER FIVE
JUST START   67

CHAPTER SIX
BUILD A BUSINESS YOU LOVE   87

CHAPTER SEVEN
THE POWER OF COMMUNITY   103

CHAPTER EIGHT
IT'S NOT THE CRITIC WHO COUNTS   121

CHAPTER NINE
FROM SURVIVING TO THRIVING   137

CHAPTER TEN
WHAT'S THE BEST THAT COULD HAPPEN?   157

CHAPTER ELEVEN
FLIP THE SCRIPT AND FORGE THE FUTURE   169

CHAPTER ONE

YOUR FIELD OF DREAMS

★

"If you build it, they will come."
— *Shoeless Joe Jackson in Field of Dreams*

Within each of our small towns and communities is our very own field of dreams, where the stirring inside of us dares to believe, *If you build it, they will come.*

If you're holding this book, I believe there's a dream inside of you, restless and ready to break free. There is a business only you can build. A town only your community can save. No one else can tell its story or share its unique perspective. There is a dream waiting to happen that the world doesn't even know it needs yet. Whatever the dream, it's there, burning in your heart, waiting for you to say yes.

And I'm here to tell you: It's time to go chase that dream.

So many of us have a dream burning inside, an idea that feels both thrilling and terrifying. Just reading these words stirs something in your soul. Maybe you want to launch a business on Main Street. Maybe you want to turn a hobby into something more. Or maybe you have a creative project to share with the world. Thinking about bringing these ideas to life seems a little scary, if we're all being honest. The idea can feel vulnerable, even risky. But what if those dreams are in your heart for a reason? What if they are meant to come alive?

For me, *Rural Revival* was a dream I never saw coming. But looking back, I see it's a dream God absolutely needed me to live out. I'll be honest, I'm not one who likes to talk about myself. I'd rather shine the light on others instead. But if I'm asking you to be brave and step boldly into your dreams, then I owe it to you to share how I found my way into living my dream. My story isn't perfect, but it's proof that the journey matters—and that yours can lead you somewhere extraordinary too.

ROOTS THAT RUN DEEP

I was born and raised on a farm in western Iowa, a patchwork of corn and soybean fields with quiet horizons stretching out from Odebolt, a rural dot on the map. Here my parents gave my siblings and I more than just a home—they handed us a way of life. On that farm, we learned how to work for our money, how to care for what mattered, and how to find purpose in stewarding the land. They also taught us to live a life of faith—to trust God in all things, especially the unknowns.

My roots are tangled deep in this Iowa soil, and I'm forever grateful for it. Even now, as I chase this business venture, those early lessons guide me and I'm still leaning on the same grit and gratitude. And no matter where I go, my roots lead me back to the farm, a quiet place to land amid the chaos of life.

SMALL TOWN MEETS BIG CITY

Like so many of you, I knew life would likely take me away from the farm, but I always dreamed of someday returning to my hometown. Growing up in rural Iowa, I think that longing was born in me. Many of you can relate. I remember the night of my high school graduation, when our class of 52 gathered at a local farm pond to celebrate. It was one of the rare times we were all together outside of school, laughing and living it up under the stars. I remember the conversations to this day—everyone saying how much they loved our small town and how they wished they could stay. Yet beneath it all lingered an unspoken truth: Unless you were tied to farming or a few other local businesses, staying wasn't an option. Most of us, me included, had to leave. That night, though, I felt the ache of wanting to make it possible to find a way back someday. And that ache never left me.

College came next. I earned a degree in public relations—a perfect fit for my skills, but a career that screamed city. Rural America didn't have public relations jobs then (I'm so glad that's not the case anymore). After graduation, I stumbled into a gig as a travel director, helping put on fancy events for Fortune 500 top earners. That job took me to amazing places and taught me the ins and outs of hospitality, but the work wasn't steady enough to build a life on. So, I traded it for a corporate advertising job. It was stable, I made new friends, and I learned a lot—but that restless feeling never left me. I remember thinking, *There's got to be more than this.* My heart still yearned for purpose—and for home.

That restlessness followed me into a new role, when I was recruited by a local church in Des Moines to be their director of communication. Church work is a whirlwind—which for me included events, digital and print communications, websites, guest services, you name it—and I juggled more than I thought possible with an incredible team by my side. I loved the people and the purpose that job gave me, yet the pull toward my small town never faded.

UNEXPECTED GIFTS

Something unexpected happened at that church, a gift I didn't recognize until later. With a limited budget and a desperate need for some new websites, I reached out to a few local companies to help, but they quoted me astronomical prices well beyond my budget. At that time Squarespace was a new platform that promised anyone could build a website.

Trust me, I'm the last person in the world who thought I would ever build a website, but desperate times call for desperate measures. I decided to block off a few days to see if I could figure out the platform and build a new website for the church. And much to my surprise, I did it! I came away with a site I was proud of. During my time there I also taught myself how to use design software, creating logos and graphics to stretch our budget further. Those skills, born out of necessity, planted seeds for a future I couldn't yet see.

Several years into that job I got a wild opportunity to start a record label with a friend of mine who was a Grammy-winning producer. Nashville was calling my name, and it was an experience I couldn't pass up. I loved working in the music industry and Nashville stole my heart—a vibrant city bursting with music, creativity, and entrepreneurial spirit everywhere I turned. If ever there was a perfect combination for me, that was it. At the same time, that job moved me even farther away from my Iowa roots, and my dream of moving back home seemed more impossible than ever.

THE SPARK OF RURAL REVIVAL

It was in Nashville that *Rural Revival* was born—not because I went looking for it, but because in a way it found me. I was surrounded by so many creative, innovative businesses, and often I'd find myself thinking, *That could work in a small town.* Driving back home to the farm in Iowa, I'd pass through so many fading rural communities, their quiet streets tugging at my heart. I mourned the thought of these places disappearing, taking with them the childhood experiences like I'd known and loved, and the families that had been rooted there for generations. I would think to myself, *These places matter. There has to be more we can do.*

One Christmas back home in Iowa, some friends and I sang at a show at *The Nineteen14*, a historic depot turned bar and grill. It belonged to my friend Jeremy Mahler—a guy who'd built businesses worldwide and decided to come back to his hometown of 250 people and build something there. I noticed the place wasn't just surviving; it was alive. That night, over the music and laughter, I said, "What Jeremy's doing is incredible. People need to know this is possible—that you can build something amazing in a small town and actually make it work." At some point in the conversation I said, "Someone should start a podcast and tell these stories." And everyone looked at me and said, "*You* should do that!"

I brushed it off. But the thought stayed with me all through Christmas break, and it kept coming up in conversation. When I got back to Nashville, I still couldn't shake the idea, so I finally said, "God, if this is You, give it a name." I can tell you exactly where I was a few weeks later when the name *Rural Revival* dropped in my mind. And in that moment, I knew God was telling me to start a podcast.

Wait! What?

STEPPING INTO THE UNKNOWN

I loved listening to podcasts, but I knew absolutely nothing about recording one or how to put it out in the world for people to listen to it. Thankfully, my music friends in Nashville stepped in—helping me get the right equipment, teaching me to record and edit, and even composing the theme music that opens every episode. It was incredible to have them help me and believe in me as I started. We all need those people in our lives.

I decided to do interviews in person so I could really experience the stories and towns I featured. At first, I interviewed my friends, releasing new episodes each week. I had no idea if anyone would listen—or how they would even find the podcast. Then, out of nowhere, people from places I'd never heard of started reaching out: *Can you help our business? Our town?* I was stunned. I'll be honest, I wasn't expecting that. I asked those people to give me a little time, and I would get back to them—and give myself a chance to figure out what I was doing. This was supposed to be a podcast, not a *lifeline*.

But what if it *could* be more?

Around that time, I heard a message about using what's in your hands to establish what's in your heart. In my hands was a career full of experience—public relations, marketing, communications, branding. Helping people tell their stories and build their brands was what I knew best. So, I started dreaming. *How could I use what's in my hands to serve these small towns and businesses?*

I took it one step at a time to see what might stick. I was willing to try anything once to find out if an idea would work. If it was a success, I would keep going down that path. If it wasn't, I would take what I could learn from it and move on to the next thing.

My first leap was a small event for entrepreneurs in Pawhuska—an Oklahoma cow town experiencing revival, largely driven by *The Pioneer Woman*'s dream and vision. I knew the setting would provide the inspiration these small business owners needed. This event was small, but the experience was powerful, and it led to larger events in the future.

Then came an online community where we met weekly to gain inspiration from guest speakers—and each other—as we chased our small-town dreams. This launched the very week COVID shut everything down. Only God could've orchestrated something already set up to connect us through Zoom—which soon became our source of community just as the world needed it most.

I leaned on those website and design skills from my church days as I started to build brands for rural businesses and towns. I know what a critical role a solid website and branding play in helping small businesses thrive and small towns revive. It had always been my dream to create a branding agency that employed people who were exclusively from small towns. Who better to serve small towns and small businesses than the people who actually live there? I knew I would have to find the right people to join me if this dream was ever meant to be.

Over time, after putting out some feelers behind the scenes, I was able to build the dream team I'd patiently waited for. And it was worth the wait. Through *Branded by Rural Revival*, we've created a rural design agency to help small businesses and small towns build amazing brands. We're living our dream, right from the heart of rural America, serving the people and places we love.

COMING HOME

As I look back on the early days of launching my dream, I now see that *Rural Revival* didn't just help revive towns and bring small town dreams to life—it also brought me full circle. In March of 2020, as the podcast really took off, I packed my things into a storage unit and decided to hit the road full-time. I could never have known that ten days later a pandemic would hit, landing me back on the family farm in Iowa. Quarantine became a gift—a sort of trial run at the life I'd always dreamed of—living on the farm, surrounded by family, in my hometown. It was the silver lining in an unexpected twist.

For many of us who've left our hometowns, there's a lingering dream of returning someday—this nostalgic vision that feels like a scene from a Hallmark movie. Yet, there's always that persisting question: Would I actually enjoy it if I took the plunge? That experience gave me the opportunity to find out, and I was surprised by how much being close to my family and being on the farm, far from the city life I'd known for years, felt deeply fulfilling. Ultimately the farm became my home base, a decision that's proven to be incredibly rewarding. I still spend plenty of time on the road, but now I get to come home to the place that's always been my truest north.

THREADS OF A BIGGER STORY

By now, you'll notice a few connecting threads woven through my journey—threads like encouraging others to pursue their dreams, build their brands, and trust that every step matters, even when it doesn't make sense. With God guiding me, I've been able to draw on experiences from my past to shape what I'm doing today. Looking back, I see how there were threads in every season that tied into the next, a living reminder of Genesis 50:20—that God works all things together for good.

I spent years wondering what my calling was. It's only in the last seven to ten years that I really started to understand and step into the divine purpose for my life. Honestly, I couldn't have mapped this path if I had tried. There's no way. My journey's been messy, beautiful, and unpredictable, full of days I cried out for *more* and moments I never dared dream possible. And I want you to know that if God can do it for me, He can do it for you too.

The different seasons of your life are so much more connected than you realize. As I reflect on my own life, I can see how a part of each season was connected to the next. When I worked that corporate job, I was also a worship leader at my church. And it was one Sunday when I was leading worship that a staff member approached me about the director of communication role they were looking to fill at the church. That job taught me website building and design—skills I'd later use. And it was because of a concert we put on at the church that I met the music producer who just happened to be traveling with the band that day. That divine connection led to a friendship, which resulted in our starting a record label together. You can start to see how it's all connected. These are just highlights; my life is full of examples like these.

Whether it's new experiences, the people you meet, being in the right place at the right time (what I like to call divine appointments), or gaining a new skill to add to your tool belt, God uses all of it to grow you and get you where you need to be.

I can also get sentimental over the lessons I learned in my hometown. I'm thankful I got away for a while to gain some perspective and start to build this dream of mine—but I'm even more thankful to be back and able to *keep* building my dream in rural America.

Your path might start in your hometown, or it might take you to distant places before circling back. Wherever it leads, I hope my story inspires you with this truth: Your dream is possible. Every broken road matters. Every twist and turn matters. Every passion in your heart matters. And through these pages, I'm here to inspire, equip, and cheer you on as you chase your small-town dream.

If you build it—they will come.

YOUR FIELD OF DREAMS

I opened this chapter reflecting on *Field of Dreams*. As an Iowa farm girl, this movie has a special place in my heart for many reasons. Set in the small town of Dyersville, Iowa, it follows Ray Kinsella, a local farmer who one night hears a mysterious voice in his cornfield saying, "If you build it, he will come." Inspired by this voice he can't ignore to pursue a dream he can hardly believe, Ray takes a leap of faith, plowing down his crops to build a baseball diamond. Everyone thought he was crazy—until people actually started to show up. Suddenly the ghosts of baseball legends began emerging from the rows of corn to play ball, and the locals started to show up to watch.

As the story unfolds, we discover this field of dreams is about much more than bringing former baseball greats out to play. It's a picture of redemption, forgiveness, and the power of faith—a second chance at dreams left unlived. "Is this heaven?" one player asks. "No," Ray replies, "it's Iowa."

Ray's field mirrors our own callings—ordinary places transformed by faith in a dream. When you look at it this way, the film becomes a narrative for answering God's call on your life—hearing His voice, following His clues, putting the pieces of the puzzle together, stepping out in faith, and watching Him meet you there. It's listening to the Holy Spirit's whisper, urging you to trust, to build, to watch God show up. At first, only a few see it. Then more come, drawn by something they can't explain. But like Ray, you must believe in the dream before it can come to life.

> *"People will come, Ray. They'll come to Iowa, for reasons they can't even fathom. They'll turn up your driveway, not knowing for sure why they're doing it. They'll arrive at your door as innocent as children and they'll find they have reserved seats right along the sideline. And they'll watch the game and it'll be as if they've dipped themselves in magic waters."*
> *- Terrence Mann in Field of Dreams*

Do you believe in your dream? Can you see your dream over your town and over your life? If so, keep reading, this journey is about to get good.

★

ACTIVATION

What is your "field of dreams"?

What threads do you see connecting different seasons of your life?

What might these threads be showing you about your future and God's call on your life?

CHAPTER TWO

ROOTS & WINGS

★

"A small town is a canvas where your wildest dreams can paint a future no city could imagine."
— *Willa Cather*

Rural America has always had a big piece of my heart, and growing up here, I knew this place was special. But it took moving away to make me realize how truly special it really is. Now that I've lived in both worlds—the cities and the small towns—I can tell you this: There's no better place to build a dream than right here, in the wild, wide-open frontier of rural America. Right here is the heartbeat of the American dream, where our small towns are ripe with potential. It's a new day, and we're standing on the edge of something extraordinary—a chance to forge a future where our towns don't just survive, but soar.

Since launching *Rural Revival*, I've witnessed a revolution reshaping the heartland. The revival of small towns is rewriting the story of rural America, fueled by remote work, affordable living, and a quality of life that cities can't match. Young professionals and dreamers are being drawn back—not to settle, but to build. They're choosing small towns, driven by a conviction that says, *This is where I belong*. And as this movement gains momentum, rural America is proving it's not a limitation; it's a superpower—and the most underestimated entrepreneurial ecosystem in the country. This is no ordinary moment—it's a rural resurgence. More than just a trend, it's a reimagining of what's possible—bringing innovation, jobs, and revitalization to our towns.

What makes rural America so special? It's the power of "small"—where one dream can transform an entire community and impact generations. From innovators turning old barns into thriving businesses to neighbors rallying to paint a mural that sparks a movement, one bold idea can rewrite a town's story. You can plant yourself deep in the community you love, with neighbors who know your name, while letting your dreams take flight, reaching heights you never thought possible. Because in small towns, your vision doesn't just lift you—it lifts everyone around you, creating a future where kids and grandkids choose to stay. This isn't just a lifestyle; it's a movement to reimagine what's possible and show the world what rural America can do.

What a time to be alive! Instead of chasing opportunities elsewhere, we're creating opportunities right here. Now it's up to us to seize those opportunities and turn potential into reality.

It's time for you to step into this moment—to plant your roots, spread your wings, and claim your place on this frontier that still seems a little bit wild. Because here, in the shadow of grain silos and sunlit Main Streets, you don't have to choose between roots and wings—you can have both.

REWRITE THE NARRATIVE

For too long, there's been an unspoken but lingering belief that if you grew up in a small town and wanted to make something of yourself—something *great*—you had to leave. Pack your bags, chase the bright lights of the city, and find success where the world feels bigger.

But when did we decide rural America wasn't enough? When did we start to believe our hometowns couldn't hold our dreams?

I believe the idea traces back to the farm crisis of the 1980s, which dealt a devastating blow and shook rural America to its core. Farms failed, jobs dried up, and communities crumbled under the weight of economic hardship. Unless you were tied to agriculture, the message became clear: Success lives somewhere else. That narrative—part reality, part self-fulfilling prophecy—cast a long shadow. Rural America became a place where big dreams felt out of reach. Staying often meant settling. Dreaming big felt like a risk you weren't supposed to take.

Decades later, the scars of that crisis still linger, but the story is changing. Rural America is no longer just a place to come from—it's a place to stay, a place to come home to, a place to build with limitless possibilities. For me, coming home to build my life and chase my dreams felt right, and I'm not alone. Many others are having the same experience. It's a homecoming that challenges the status quo, proving that small towns can be the foundation for big dreams. Because as it turns out, rural America is a place where we can have roots and wings, a place where we're not just allowed to dream again—it's a place we're *called* to.

SOMEBODY SHOULD...

Walk into any small-town coffee shop or diner, and you'll hear it—the chatter of local news mixed with some opinions about the community. "Somebody should open a bakery." "Somebody should fix up that old storefront." "Somebody should start a summer celebration." We've all said it, or at least nodded along. But here's the question: *Who's "somebody"?*

Mike McCartney, Director of the *Pawhuska Chamber of Commerce*, nailed it on my podcast. He heard the same chorus of "you should" and "why don't they" in his town, until one day he turned to another leader in town, Kathy Ross, and said, "Wait—we're 'they.' We need to do something." So, they did. They launched *The Shoppes at Townmaker Square*, restoring three historic buildings, transforming them into business incubators, and bringing eighteen new businesses to Pawhuska's Main Street. Eighteen new dreams, eighteen new sparks of life in their community—all because they stopped waiting for "somebody" and stepped up.

Similarly, Matt Floyd of *Matt's Bat* has never viewed it as a city's responsibility to bring fun, cool things to a town. Instead, he offers, "If you want something, let's go do it. Figure out a way you can make it happen." If the community wants it, it'll work—if not, it wasn't meant to be. Like my friend Melissa Nelson of *Hungry Canyon* and *Rural Route Ramble* says, "If you want cool things in your small town, you have to do cool things." This mindset is exactly what turns sleepy towns and empty storefronts into opportunities.

Your town's waiting for you to be that somebody. That idea you keep tossing around—maybe a café, a boutique, or a fun new event—could be the spark your community needs. You don't need permission or a perfect plan. You just need to decide you're that somebody. Your dream isn't just a wish; it's a call to action. Stop waiting for someone else to make it happen. Your town needs your courage, your vision, right now. So, what's that "somebody should" idea in your heart? It's time to run with it—because that somebody is you.

SPARKS OF REVIVAL

For every town experiencing a revival, you'll find behind that revival is a visionary. I've noticed every thriving small town has this one vital ingredient. These trailblazers see beyond what *is*—they envision what *could be*. With wild ideas and relentless optimism, they're transforming vacant Main Streets into launchpads for dreams, drowning out doubt with possibility in the process. As Haley Miles, the photographer behind *Sandhills Blue*, says, "The opportunity here is way bigger than people make it out to be. Part of that means you have to create your own opportunity. But that doesn't mean it's not here." Her words are a rallying cry: Pick up your tools and start building! One dream, one risk, can wake up an entire town.

Across rural America, visionaries are proving what's possible. When Heather and Justin Slack arrived in their small town of Harrington, Washington, they saw possibility where others saw decline. "Instead of seeing old run-down buildings and nothing happening here," Heather recalls, "we thought, *This is a really great place to raise a family... there's a ton of opportunity here.*"

They didn't just settle—they ignited change. They opened *The Post & Office*, a small-town gathering space complete with a full-service coffee shop, gift store, and shared workspace. "We ended up being like an ignition switch or a spark," Justin adds. "People saw what could be done." One family's vision helped shift a town's perception, proving that potential often hides in plain sight.

Just down the street, Jerry and Karen Allen are reviving *Hotel Lincoln—The Electric Hotel*, a 1902 landmark that had fallen into disrepair. With grit and determination, they're restoring it as a cornerstone for Harrington's future. "This town has incredible assets," Karen says. "They're worth preserving and building upon." Their efforts are cultivating a vibrant environment for residents and entrepreneurs alike.

In Red Oak, Iowa, Jill and Daric O'Neal are also dreaming big. Jill's home decor store, *J.Mercantile*, is more than a business—it's a commitment to progress. "We are continually dreaming, asking, 'What can we do next? What does our town need?'" Jill says. Daric adds, "It just takes a few people to step up and take the lead." As some of their town's biggest cheerleaders, they show that revival begins with those who dare to blaze the trail.

Morgann McCoy Boettner of *A Well Worn Story* adds, "It only takes one awesome business to then help other local businesses out, and you can grow a great downtown." A single café, boutique, or brewery can spark a chain reaction, turning quiet streets into bustling hubs. Small isn't insignificant—it's powerful when fueled by heart and collaboration.

As Joni Nash, former director of the *Pawhuska Chamber of Commerce* says of her once-quiet town, now bustling with tourists: "If it can happen here, it can happen anywhere. There's so many towns that have the same ingredients. You've just gotta be creative."

When you look at a small-town Main Street with vacant, dilapidated buildings, what do you see? Decay? Or, like me, do you see opportunity? Possibility? These buildings are more than monuments to the past—they're a chance to preserve history while shaping the future. They call us to dream big in small places, to ignite a revival that transforms communities far beyond a single street.

A BLANK CANVAS

Small towns offer a rare gift, a blank canvas where dreamers can paint their visions without the constraints of crowded cities. Here, opportunity rewards those who are willing to step up and act. Doing so is not about waiting for change, it's about making it happen, one idea at a time. So, if you dream of a brick and mortar, a place where your dream can come to life, you're in luck—because most of our small towns are brimming with historic buildings or vacant lots, just waiting for someone to come in and show a little TLC.

In McIntosh, Minnesota, Andrea Stordahl of *Minnesota Rust* saw potential where others saw a dying town. "To me there's just so much magic in these old buildings and these renovations. And I don't mean to make them sound like they're easy, they're not. But they're really fun," says Andrea, a self-titled "accidental entrepreneur."

She started by renovating a historic downtown building to house her growing vintage business. In the beginning she was met with her fair share of skepticism. "'Businesses don't survive here, Andrea. This town is dying.' I heard that a lot. Not from bad people, but from people who had been living there for so long—it's like their hearts were broken. They were a little upset that they'd seen so many things fail."

But *Minnesota Rust* provided the spark the town needed. After the shop took off, she and her husband, Bryce, decided to go all in with revitalizing their downtown to create a place where their kids can make memories and be proud to come home to. They have now renovated six downtown buildings and brought in a handful of new businesses—collectively branding themselves as *The Shoppes of McIntosh*. Together they promote McIntosh's retail scene and pool their resources for marketing, events, sourcing, staffing, and more. One dream, one risk, can awaken an entire town.

In Edelstein, Illinois, a pop-up shop called *Here and Gone Mercantile* brought a most unexpected vision to life, proving you can take any old building and make it support your vision. Paige Ehnle Heaton of *No Roots Boots* gathered a few of her small business friends and created an experience like the town has never seen—for one day only. Over the course of a month, these friends took a vacant building—a dusty, dirty old general store—and transformed into a hopping little shop. As Paige described it, "For that one day, we breathed life back into our little town and that big old building—full of one-of-a-kind finds, curated clothes, boots, funky art, and the best people any small-town dreamer could ask for."

"Watching our risk and vision come to life was truly a dream," Paige says. Friends drove three hours to support it, a testament to the pull of small-town dreams. "There is no way I could adequately say thank you," she adds, her gratitude spilling over at the wonder of a dream realized. It's a fleeting moment that lingers—a reminder that the opportunity is there in our small towns if we are brave enough to seek it out.

A fulfilled dream doesn't always come easy, as many of us have experienced. Sometimes people don't want to get rid of their buildings—not because they're using them, but because they're sentimental or they fear change. Yes, we have an attachment to these buildings in our small towns, but we also have a responsibility to ensure they remain places for future opportunities, not just spaces for storage or nostalgic memories.

CONVERGE THE OLD WITH THE NEW

Rural America's small towns are more than just places—they're stories etched in brick and timber, waiting to be retold. Our historic buildings, weathered storefronts, and empty lots aren't remnants to be discarded; they can be the foundation for a vibrant future. Every community has its own pulse, its own vision for what's next. Some towns have lost their old structures, leaving new construction as the only path forward. Others hold tight to their historic buildings, hoping to weave the past into something vibrant and lasting. The opportunity lies in bridging the past with the future—capturing the soul of Main Street while sparking revival through fresh ideas.

By embracing these opportunities, we can protect the historical integrity of our existing structures while cohesively blending historic elements into new storefronts. This approach creates a vital connection between past and present, preserving and enriching the timeless charm of our town's Main Street for future generations.

I saw this vision come to life at Freshfields Village on Kiawah Island in the heart of South Carolina's Lowcountry. Built from the ground up, this village isn't old, but it feels like it's been there forever. Every detail—a barrel-topped building, an old-style gas station, a feed-and-seed-inspired grocery, even a windmill—evokes the charm of a small town, minutes from the beach. It's a deliberate nod to rural roots, designed to feel like home. My mind raced with ideas for our towns, where we already have the real thing: historic buildings begging for new life.

"In a small place, our historic buildings are one of our only natural resources," says Angela Harrington, owner of *Hotel Grinnell*, a former school building turned boutique hotel in Grinnell, Iowa. Some may say we can't afford to keep these buildings, but maybe instead we should ask, *Can our small towns can afford to lose them?* Darin Smith of *Arch Icon Development* in Woodbine, Iowa, adds a practical perspective: "It's going to cost more to rebuild, and [new buildings] have no significance to the community." These existing structures aren't just history—they're the foundation for what's next.

When we lose these buildings, we lose more than bricks. Author Darcy Maulsby reflected on the demolition of a school in Pomeroy, Iowa: "An abandoned chair. An overturned wastebasket. A jumbled pile of radiators. These scenes always hurt my heart. I know we can't save every old building, nor should we. Yet these losses don't point to growth and progress. What will these towns look like in ten years?" Her words stay with us, urging us to act. Oftentimes saving an old building is far more likely than replacing it with something new—and far more meaningful.

"There are far too many small towns with boarded up, darling buildings that just sit vacant," says Jasmin Stidham of *Stidham Outfitters*. These buildings are not liabilities—they're opportunities. "Work with your local community or economic development group to open the doors and dust off the old shelves and just do a pop up—something that would get people thinking about what Main Street businesses might look like and how big of an impact it truly has on a small community." Explore new possibilities and watch how one spark can shift how your community sees itself. Not sure where to start? Survey people in your town—ask what they want. You can grab a free survey template at ruralrevival.co/townsurvey to guide your efforts.

Small towns thrive when you weave the past into the future. Their historic spaces and empty lots are keys to revival—blank canvases for your vision, your business, your legacy. Maybe it's time to step into the challenge, pour your heart into those weathered walls, and build something that will inspire your community for generations to come.

THE HEART AND SOUL OF SMALL TOWNS

Small towns are far more than dots on a map—they're living stories shaped by deep-rooted ties, shared histories, and neighbors who invest in each other. The soul of these communities lies in their people. Relationships aren't fleeting transactions; they're the result of bonds forged over decades. Here, one big dream doesn't just build a business, it breathes life into the heart of a town.

Take Joni Nash, who relocated to serve as the director of the *Pawhuska Chamber of Commerce*. "I'm thankful that I had the audacity to step out and invest in this community because this community has invested in me, received me, and loved me." Her words capture the promise of small-town life: You give to the town, and the town gives back tenfold. That same promise drove Bonnie and Theo Ramsey to leave a successful life in St. Louis and return to Bonnie's hometown of Lenox, Iowa. "We had the jobs and house we never thought we'd get," she says, "but I realized none of that mattered. It was the people, the community I missed. We wanted to come back and give back." That longing inspired *Ramsey's Market*, a grocery store that's not just a business but a gathering place that offers fresh goods and entertainment to a town eager for both.

Callie Taylor Dayton, an economic developer and co-owner of *May Tree Farm*, also embraces the same promise. "Growing up in agriculture taught me that small can be impactful," she says. By day, she champions her community's growth. On weekends, she pours her heart into her family's Christmas tree farm. "When a town is proud of who they are, they rally around you," she adds. That pride turns dreams into reality, whether it's a farm or a new venture, proving that starting small doesn't mean dreaming small. Sandy Schubert, who opened *Hedgie's Books* in Bedford, Iowa, felt that sense of pride too. A newcomer embraced by her town, she says, "I love the brick streets, the unique architecture, the distance from big cities. But mostly, I love the people. They've made this home." Her bookstore isn't just a shop—it's a testament to a community that welcomes and uplifts.

"Small communities are made of really good people," Joni Nash reflects, "people who care for each other because they've done life together for generations." This isn't nostalgia—it's a dynamic strength that sets rural America apart. It's why Josh Scheutzow and his wife, of *The Kilbourne Project*, bet their life savings on their town, saying, "We believe in small town neighbors taking care of each other."

In rural America, your dream isn't just yours—it's a gift to your community, creating jobs, town pride, and a future where the next generation wants to stay. This is the heart and soul of a small town: a place where people with big hearts rally around you, and your courage to dream can ignite inspiration throughout the entire community. As Richard Russo writes, "People in small towns, much more than in cities, share a destiny." Your dreams gain wings when carried on the shoulders of those who know your name and champion your success.

THE POWER OF SMALL

Small towns offer an opportunity that's hard to shake—a call to simplicity, connection, and the thrill of building something real. For those of us who have chosen to make these small places home, we realize rural America offers a canvas for dreams in a way big cities often can't, where relationships endure and one bold move can lift everyone up. Instead of looking at what's missing—we're focusing on what's possible. That shift from doubt to pride is the heartbeat of revival, and it's beating stronger every day.

Rural America's simplicity is what so many crave. Tourism has caught on too, perhaps fueled by Hallmark Christmas movies that paint quaint downtowns as the backdrop for romance and a real quality-of-life experience. But beyond the postcard image lies a deeper truth: The power of *small* is being rediscovered. One thriving business can revive a Main Street. One restored building can transform decline into possibility. One wild dream can wake up a town.

Your journey—whether you stayed in rural America, chose to return after dreaming of bigger and better, or are new to small-town life—mirrors so many of these stories. They prove that big dreams don't always need a big stage, that success doesn't always mean leaving, and that the good life might just be right where you started. Success begins with putting creativity into action—taking a risk, building something that matters, and watching a community show up for it. These small towns might not have the shiny allure of cities, but they've got something better—heart, grit, and endless potential.

So, why think big when you can think *small*? Plant your roots, rally your people, and start building a life that you love. In rural America, the biggest adventures don't need a sprawling map—just a daring heart, a place to call home, and the courage to build a life that you love.

Access our free town survey template available for download at ruralrevival.co/townsurvey.

37

★

ACTIVATION

What resonates with you most about "the power of small"?

How are you called to have roots and wings in your small town?

How do you honor the history of your town while embracing new ideas for its future?

CHAPTER THREE

DARE TO DREAM AGAIN

★

*"All our dreams can come true if we
have the courage to pursue them."*
— Walt Disney

There's something about chasing a wild, seemingly impossible dream that sets a soul on fire. For many of us in small towns, that dream often takes the shape of entrepreneurship—a chance to build something uniquely ours. Our dreams might seem unrealistic, even irresponsible to others. But to us? They feel like destiny. Welcome to the big dream world of small-town entrepreneurship.

Running my own business has let me live life on my terms—true to my values, my identity, and my desire to make a difference. It's given me a career that supported me in the move back to my hometown and sent me across the country to share stories about your hometowns. Most importantly, it's allowed me to help other small-town dreamers pursue their dreams. Some may call our businesses small, but our passion, courage, and vision? Anything but. Nothing about these qualities feels small to me at all.

This entrepreneurial adventure has given me a lot of freedom and purpose, and I want that for you too.

ARE YOU SETTLING?

We're all on a journey together, uncovering the dreams and callings God has placed in our hearts—right here in these rural places where He's planted us.

Part of my role with *Rural Revival* is to call you up and call you out—to help you step into the life God created you for. That means encouragement and equipping through things like trainings and events, but it also means asking the hard questions: *Where in your life are you settling for less instead of pursuing what you truly dream of?*

Maybe you've sensed a calling for your life, a tug towards something greater. Maybe you feel stuck or unsettled, and you crave change. You might be in a season of good things—really good things—yet you feel a divine discontent, a tension between your current work and living out your purpose. Not that where you are isn't good—but is it the best for your life? Deep down, you know there's more.

God's whispering, *Don't settle here. I've got greater things for you.*

DIG UP THE DREAM

If you're craving a new season, feeling stuck in your business, or holding an unfulfilled dream, pause and ask, *What do I truly want?* Be honest. What's that idea you can't shake? The vision you keep circling back to, wondering, *Could this work?* Dreaming means stepping into the unknown, leaving the comfort of the familiar. It's scary, but it's where God often whispers, *There's more.*

Belle Golden, owner of *Belle's Flower Truck* in Tifton, Georgia, knows this truth, having turned her vision of a mobile flower shop into reality. "Dreams give you something to strive for," she reflects. "Every day, I'm working toward something, even if I don't know exactly what it is. Dreams are always valid, always important. You should never feel they aren't reachable— because they are." Her words remind us that our dreams, no matter how vague or distant, are worth pursuing—especially in small towns where our dreams matter more than we know.

Mikaela Endress and her best friend, Kami Stahl, turned a whimsical dream into *Kamaela's Kreamery*, an ice cream truck that brightens their community. "I've always been a dreamer," Mikaela says. "This showed me nothing is too far out of reach. If I can make my four-year-old dream of an ice cream truck come true, what can't I do?"

Kami, a self-described realist, had her own breakthrough. "I used to think big dreams weren't practical, but this taught me that with hard work, you can do anything." Their story is a testament to the power of small-town dreams. Whimsical or practical, they're within reach if we dare to go after them.

Maybe you've chased a dream before and watched it soar, or maybe it slipped away, leaving scars of disappointment. Perhaps life's challenges have dimmed your spark, making it hard to imagine what's possible. Wherever you stand, hear this: It's never too late to dream again. Your small town is the perfect place to start. Those weathered Main Streets and big-hearted neighbors are ready to rally around your vision and breathe life into your small town. As Mikaela and Kami show, no dream is too big or too small when you've got the grit and courage to make it real.

So, dig up that dream. Step boldly into what's next. And dare to dream again.

WHAT IF?

Dreaming is like a muscle—the more you use it, the stronger it gets. So, let's get practical. I want you to clear your mind for a moment. If you can, close your eyes. Take a deep breath. And let me ask you: What's that dream in your heart? The one you buried under the weight of life, the one that feels so far off you're not sure it's worth chasing anymore. What is it? (If you need to, pause here and give yourself time to think.)

Now, let's play a little game of *what if*. Ask yourself:

What if it's not too late to realize my dream?
What if that dream isn't dead?
What if I started chasing it again?
What if it could work right here?
What if God placed this dream in me for a reason?
What if this dream changed my town, my life, everything?
What if I was made for this dream?

Feel that? That's the thrill of possibility. It's hope waking up. And I'm here to tell you that just because you live in a small town doesn't mean your dreams have to be small. I believe in you, and I know your dream is possible—not only because I've lived it, but because so many around me have lived it too. While I know there are no guarantees of success, I don't believe you'll regret exploring your dream more, betting on yourself, and having faith to believe in the dreams God has placed in you. Because your dream isn't just for you—others need you to live it too.

SHATTER THE LIES AND THE LIMITING BELIEFS

Sometimes, for us to really dream big, we must confront the lies and the limiting beliefs that have kept us small, holding us back from stepping into the greatness that our lives were meant for.

In small towns, there are subtle but powerful doubts that creep in: *I can't make a big impact here. There aren't enough people. Big things don't happen in places like this.* Or worse: *What will people say? They'll think this idea is crazy.*

These lies aim to steal your vision and keep you small. I've seen it time and again working with rural communities—people feel isolated, believing their dreams can't thrive locally. Oftentimes, the fear of what others might think overshadows their courage to step out. We've all wrestled with these feelings. It's tough not to settle when we see people around us who seem to have done just that. We start to think, *Well, that's just the way it is.* But what if God never meant for it to be this way? Many people around us have settled when they were never meant to.

This is where we must draw a line in the sand. If we're going to step into all that we were created for, we must leave those fears and doubts behind. It's time to dream again—and we can't let these limiting beliefs hold us back any longer. It's time to reframe our thinking, to move out of a place of lack and survival and into a place of hope and vision.

You're not stuck. You're *positioned*—right where you are, in your small town, on your farm, in your rural corner of the world —for this exact moment. So, let's confront some of the lies and limiting beliefs that cause us to settle for less and then replace them with the truth.

Lie: It's too late.

Truth: It's *never* too late to pursue your passions. In fact it's always the right time if you are willing to sacrifice to see them come to fruition.

We've been sold the story that if we haven't "made it" by age 30, we've somehow missed the boat. That midlife is about slowing down, not starting up. That our best ideas belong to a younger version of ourselves.

But stories from *Rural Revival* prove otherwise. People have launched businesses, reshaped communities, and chased dreams at all ages. They didn't listen to the "too late" narrative. They believed in themselves and the dream God placed in them, and the world is better for it.

Here are some real-world examples from names you might recognize that further support this idea:

- Taylor Sheridan (writer of *Yellowstone, 1883, 1923*) gave up everything at age 40 to become a screenwriter.
- Vera Wang made her first wedding dress at age 40.
- Sam Walton opened his first *Walmart* at age 44.
- Julia Child published her first cookbook at age 49.
- Martha Stewart started *Martha Stewart Living* at age 56.
- Colonel Harland Sanders launched *Kentucky Fried Chicken* at age 62.
- Laura Ingalls Wilder began writing the *Little House on the Prairie* books at age 65.
- Duncan Hines introduced his boxed cake mixes at age 73.

What if these people had believed it was too late? They would have missed their calling. What are you not sharing with the world that you *know* is inside you to share? If there's something tugging at your heart—a dream, an idea, a quiet whisper to do things differently—this is your reminder.

You're not too late. You're right on time.

Lie: I can't do that because I didn't go to college.

Truth: College isn't the only path to success, especially in small towns. College is valuable for certain careers—thank goodness my doctor spent years studying!—but it's not the only way to build a fulfilling life. Alternatives such as trade schools, apprenticeships, or entrepreneurship can often align better with small-town opportunities and hands-on learners.

Personally, I went to college because that was the expected next step. But I found I learned more from real-world experience than from textbooks. My public relations degree was geared for city jobs, and back then, working a job like that in a rural area seemed impossible. This is not the case today. Whether it's PR, tech, consulting, or beyond, you can live in a small town and thrive in almost any field.

Opportunity is ripe in our small towns—we have this blank canvas just waiting for young dreamers and entrepreneurs. Sure, go get a college degree if that's what you need, but then come back here and open a business, or work a remote job from here. Take a chance on rural America, because rural America is worth betting on in so many ways. The possibilities are endless.

And if college wasn't your path? Trust that was for a reason. Because college may have made you into someone or something you were never meant to be.

Lie: That's not what I went to college for. Or, that's not what my expertise is in.

Truth: You are not limited to your college major, and your past experience doesn't define your future. In today's world, you don't have to pick something and do that for the rest of your life, unless you choose to. You have options—even in a small town.

As you'll discover in this book or through the *Rural Revival* podcast, many people pursued dreams that had nothing to do with their background, training, or college degree, and it was the best thing that ever happened to them. Just look at Jaime England at *The Market Place* or Jessi Mason at *The Market & Mill*. Both are thriving in businesses that have nothing to do with their education or expertise. (You'll learn more about these two in the chapters ahead.)

And you might be surprised how skills and experiences from your past—whether from school, work, or life—were a training ground. As you follow the path God has for your life, those seemingly unrelated skills and moments just might become the foundation for your success.

Lie: I don't know how to run a business.

Truth: No one starts out knowing everything—success is a process of learning as you go. At the end of the day, there is no tried and true path to success in business. Each business has its own unique opportunities and challenges, and we get to figure them out in real time.

As an entrepreneur I am constantly learning—listening to podcasts, diving into other people's stories of success and failure, and seeking out trainings to expand my skills. The internet is a goldmine of knowledge, from AI to YouTube tutorials to online resources. I've taught myself things I never imagined I could do, such as building websites or using technology to streamline my business—skills I didn't have a decade ago. All of this has helped me on my journey, and if I can figure it out, so can you.

Don't tell yourself you can't. Jump in, embrace the learning curve, and connect with mentors who are a few steps ahead. Resources such as our *Rural Revival* Dream Builder trainings and consulting services will guide you along the way too. Your business journey starts with a single step—take it!

Lie: I don't have the confidence to do this.

Truth: It's not about confidence as much as it's about courage. We're all intimidated by the unknown, whether launching a business, trying something new, or stepping into uncharted territory. We wait for the perfect time, or we tell ourselves, *As soon as I feel more confident, I'll do it.* But we will never feel more confident until we do it.

You've probably heard the saying, "Sometimes all it takes is twenty seconds of insane courage." That one brief, bold action can change everything. When you break your fears into small, manageable steps, suddenly the impossible feels within reach. You don't need confidence to pursue your calling; you just need courage. Be brave, step out, and watch your confidence grow with every move you make.

Lie: That's not a "real" job.

Truth: A job's worth isn't measured by a timecard or a benefits package—it's defined by its impact. Entrepreneurs, freelancers, and small business owners often pour far more than forty hours a week into their work, but they do it on their terms. They solve problems, create value, and craft lives of purpose with schedules that fit their lives. Whether they start their day at

10 a.m. or work late into the night, that flexibility is their superpower, not a weakness.

A "real" job isn't defined by an outdated expectation of cubicles and 401(k)s. It's about hustle, passion, and making a difference. In a world where the internet brings endless possibilities, we should celebrate these dynamic career paths that bring freedom and purpose to small towns and beyond.

Lie: No one in my family has done this. Or, it's not the family business.

Truth: In small towns or tight-knit families, the weight of tradition can feel immense. Family businesses, often passed down through generations, come with expectations to keep the legacy alive. But what happens when your heart isn't in the family business? What if you feel called to a different path?

Navigating this tension is tough. The pressure to uphold family tradition can clash with your personal dreams, creating a painful dilemma. If you find yourself in this position, here are some options to consider:

Approach your family with honesty and respect. Ask for their blessing to explore other possible career paths and set a clear timeline for this exploration. Emphasize that you're not saying no to the family business outright—you're simply seeking clarity about your calling. You need some time to figure out if the family business really is for you.

If they're not open to that, I realize this puts you in a very difficult position. This is where you must weigh your options and make a choice. Are you willing to sacrifice the dreams in your heart to continue living your family's dreams? Is there a way you could grow to be passionate about the family business, perhaps with some changes in place? Or is it time to step away from the family business to pursue the dream God put in you?

There is no easy answer to these questions, but at the end of the day, you have to live your life for *you*. It may not be your family's dream for you, but I pray you have the courage to pursue what God put in *your* heart. If you do decide to step away, I hope your family will someday realize this was the best decision for you and those around you. It may take some time, but don't give up hope. And who knows, if you step away, it may open opportunities for others in your community to come into the family business—a potential win for everyone.

Lie: What I'm doing now is good enough.

Truth: Good is often the enemy of great. When you settle for "good enough," you risk missing the extraordinary purpose you're meant to fulfill. The comfort of good things—like safe routines and familiar roles—can quietly distract you from the great things calling your heart. Years can slip by, filled with good deeds and steady progress, yet leave you longing for the impact you were born to make. Dig deep and find the courage to believe for more. Don't let "good enough" keep you from the great things God has waiting for you.

Lie: That won't work in a small town.

Truth: Where you are is where you're called. No matter where you're living right now in your corner of rural America, this is where God has you for this specific moment in time. And for many of you, it's where you'll stay. I hope you'll see your rural location for exactly what it is—not a limitation, but a gift.

The truth is, where you live doesn't disqualify you from the dreams in your heart. Your address doesn't cancel your calling. Your stage of life—young or old, starting out or winding down—doesn't take away your purpose. If God orders your steps—and I believe He does—then He knows exactly where you are. He planted that dream in you, and He's got a plan for you to live it out *right where you are.*

You're not here by chance—God chose you for a unique destiny, perfectly designed for this very moment. As Esther 4:14 reminds us, *perhaps this is the moment for which you were created.* This is your moment to embrace your God-given purpose and ignite change. This is your time to dream again, to step boldly into the divine assignment He's clarifying for you. And as you do, your dream will have a ripple effect in your community and the lives of others, if you are brave enough to chase it.

Where you are is where God is calling you to shine. So, take your dream and run with it. Go light up the world around you— right where you are.

It's time to silence the lies and break free from the limiting beliefs that have held you back for too long. Each doubt you've confronted—whether it's "I'm too late," "I don't know enough," or "This won't work here"—is a step toward reclaiming your God-given purpose. In your small town, on your farm or ranch, or in your rural corner of the world, you're not confined by your circumstances—you're called to transform them. Your dreams are not too big, too late, or too out of reach. They're the spark God placed in you to ignite change, right where you stand. So, rise up, take that courageous first step, and trust that the path to greatness begins with believing the truth that *you were made for this moment.*

BET ON YOURSELF

One of the thrills of being an entrepreneur is getting to bet on yourself—and knowing you *have* to. You've got to believe you *can* do this, because you absolutely can. Every guest on my podcast proves that regular people from small towns can chase their dreams and make them real.

Your dream to start a business, to live with purpose, isn't crazy—it's courageous. While others settle for soul-draining jobs, working for bosses they don't respect or companies they don't believe in, you dare to break free and build something that ignites your soul.

I know the feeling of being stuck. For years, I poured my energy into corporate America, building someone else's vision while a restless tug whispered, *This isn't it.* I didn't know what "it" was, but I knew there was more. If you're reading my words and feel that same pull—that dream you can't shake—you're not alone. That's your calling, knocking at your door. When I finally took the leap into entrepreneurship, leaving behind stability and all the expertise I had gained, it was scary. No guaranteed income, no clear path. But it was the best decision I ever made. I discovered I was made for my dream, and if that resonates with you, you might be made for your dream too.

Michelle Myers felt that same call. Starting *Dirt Road Candle Co.* in her tiny kitchen in 2019, she balanced a full-time job as a grain buyer, pouring candles late into the night, pausing friendships, and pushing through doubts. "I felt crazy," she admits, "but I knew this is what I was supposed to do." Today, her business has outgrown the shed she built for it. It is now bursting with possibility and providing jobs for others. Her story shows what's possible when you bet on yourself.

The truth is, I regret not stepping out sooner. My corporate years taught me skills I use now, and yet they also delayed my purpose. Please don't make my mistake. If you feel that tug, don't wait another year. The time will pass anyway, so why not spend it building something you love? You don't need to scale up overnight or aim for unicorn status. Start small—with a side hustle, a single product, a tiny storefront, or a trailer. Stay true to your *why*—your God-given purpose—rather than striving for growth.

Betting on yourself means going all in—no backup plan. I used to think, *Maybe Rural Revival is just a hobby. Maybe I'll need to go back to corporate.* But I realized a backup plan is a crutch. If you're always looking over your shoulder at what could go wrong or what might happen if you fail, you're not fully committed to your dream. My mindset had to shift from "What if I fail?" to "There's only Plan A. I'll commit to making this work because it's my purpose, my calling." And when doubt creeps in—because it will—surround yourself with supporters who will remind you why you started and keep you focused on the vision.

This is your moment. You're living in a time when rural America is ripe for big dreams. The internet, social media, and your unique skills make anything possible—right where you are. So, take that risk. Bet on yourself. Because you are worth betting on.

YOUR DREAM IGNITES HOPE

Imagine standing on your small town's Main Street or a quiet dirt road by your farm, feeling that stirring in your soul—the dream God planted in your heart. It's not just a fleeting thought; it's a divine invitation to step into something greater. Right now, in this very moment, you're exactly where you're meant to be to make that dream come alive. But that first step is yours.

What's holding you back? The fear of failure? The weight of past disappointments? The nagging thought, *Who am I to do this?* Let me assure you that you're the exact person God chose for this. When you dare to dream, you're not just transforming your life—you're showing others what's possible. That coffee shop you've envisioned, that community event you've dreamed of, that wild idea you've tucked away—it's time to bring it to life. Trust the dream God gave you. It's bigger than you imagine, and it's meant to bless those around you.

Here's your challenge: Take a moment to sit with your dream. Grab a notebook or close your eyes and go through the activation questions below. Find out, *What's the dream I've been afraid to chase? How could it bless my town—and me?* Write down one brave step you can take this week—maybe research a business idea, reach out to a mentor, or pray for clarity and courage. Then, take that step. It doesn't need to be perfect; it just needs to be your step. Because when you move, God moves with you, and your life and your community will feel the impact.

This is your moment. Dare to dream again. Step boldly into the purpose God has placed in you. Your small town isn't a limit —it's your launchpad. Your courage to dream again can awaken your purpose and create a ripple of possibility and hope that transforms your community—because where you are is exactly where you're called to shine!

Explore our Dream Builder trainings at ruralrevival.co/learn.

Schedule a strategic planning session at ruralrevival.co/strategicplanning.

★

ACTIVATION

Do you believe what you're experiencing right now is God's best for you?

Where in your life or business are you settling for "good enough"?

What's the one dream you've been afraid to name? How could chasing that dream bless your town? How could it bless you?

What lie or limiting belief is holding you back, and what truth can you replace it with to move forward?

If you were the first to boldly chase your dream, who in your town or circle might be inspired to pursue their own dream? How does this possibility motivate you to take action?

CHAPTER FOUR

IT'S NOT JUST ABOUT YOU

★

"Your purpose is not the thing you do. It is the thing that happens in others when you do what you do."
— Dr. Caroline Leaf

You get one life. Just one. If you break it down, the average lifespan is about 4,000 weeks. That's a fleeting number when you think about it, a stark reminder that every moment counts. So, what are you going to do with your one wild and precious life?

You were created with a purpose—a unique calling that's yours to fulfill. Those big dreams tugging at your heart, the ideas keeping you up at night? They're not random. They're part of a divine blueprint, designed not just for you but for the impact you're meant to have on others. Your purpose isn't your job title, your to-do list, or even your biggest accomplishment. It's the contribution you were created to make to the world, and when you live it out, it ignites a spark in others and pulls something great out of them.

I don't know about you, but I want to live with as much purpose as possible because I want to help impact as many people as possible. I want to know that I poured out every dream God put in my heart, that He was able to use my life to touch others. Pastor Mike Todd puts it powerfully:

> One thing about me is, *I will die empty.* Let me explain, as Myles Munroe once said: the wealthiest place in the world is the cemetery. There lies businesses that need started up, songs that were never written, books that were never penned, problems that were never solved, cures that were never discovered, and purposes that were never fulfilled because people never stepped out in crazy faith to see what God could do. I will not let my fear limit God because of what others think or be confined to the box that's usually associated with my other responsibilities. Therefore, I will die empty. Everything that God has given me I will release because it's not just for me!

Too many people let fear or doubt keep their gifts buried. But not you. You were born with something inside that refuses to settle for average, something that knows you were destined to make a difference using your unique talents, experiences, and passions.

So, what's holding you back? And more importantly, what are you going to do about it?

THE QUESTION THAT SHAPES US

We've been asked this question from an early age: *What do you want to be when you grow up?* For some, the answer is crystal clear. But for me, the path wasn't so obvious. There were a lot of things I could be, things I could learn and probably be good at, but no one thing stood out to me. It felt impossible to choose just one.

I remember as high school graduation neared, I faced the daunting task of trying to decide my future career path so it could be printed in the commencement program below my picture and name. I waited until the last day to submit my answer because I just didn't know. This also explains why I switched majors five times in college. (Don't worry, I still graduated in four years, much to my parents' relief!) The truth is, there just wasn't a glaringly obvious answer to that question for me.

My brother was the exact opposite. He knew he wanted to be a farmer from the moment he could talk. I've always been a little envious of him for that. (If only it could be that easy, right?) His eyes would light up at anything to do with farming, and all these years later, that has never stopped. He's now a fifth-generation farmer who is truly living out his purpose, and I love getting to have a front row seat to it all.

But for me? I think that entrepreneurial spirit has always been in me, it just took a while to find it. After watching my parents and grandparents work hard and take risks to get ahead in life, deep down I craved that entrepreneurial freedom to build something of my own—to take chances, call my own shots, and own both my successes and failures. I wanted the flexibility to work hard yet also make my own schedule. But doing what? What was I made for?

It wasn't until *Rural Revival* started gaining traction that for the first time in my life, I felt like I was stepping into my "sweet spot"—doing something I was made to do. Championing small towns, shining a light on rural businesses, and helping people chase their dreams set my soul on fire. Looking back, I realize this passion had always been there—woven through lunch conversations, coffee meetings, and moments of inspiring others to step into their purpose. I bet your life holds similar hints, those small whispers of what you're meant to do.

So, let me ask you: *What do you want to be when you grow up?* Whether you've known your calling since kindergarten or you're still searching, I can promise you this: Your life will never lack meaning if you are focused on the value you can provide for others—and that's life on purpose. Now let's uncover what this looks like for you.

TAKE INVENTORY

If you're going to dream, you've first got to understand your purpose and how your dreams align with that purpose. Because most likely, the two are tied together. So, how do you discover your purpose? It starts with taking inventory of who you are and what makes you come alive. Your purpose lies at the intersection of your passion, burden, gifts, and experiences. Here are some keys that helped me uncover my purpose—and they can guide you too. Grab a pen, find a quiet spot, and let's dig in.

Passion
What stirs your heart? What gets you excited? What could you talk about for hours? In a busy world, it's easy to lose sight of this. Ask yourself these questions: *What do I love to do? What makes me come alive? If money weren't an issue, how would I spend my time?* Your passion is the fire that points to your purpose.

Burden

What breaks your heart? What tugs at you until you have to act? Lou Engle says, "Pay attention to your tears and your dreams, because they're pointing to your destiny." Think of someone you know who's living their purpose. Often, it ties back to a burden they couldn't ignore—a dream that answered a need in their heart. Your burden often reveals the problem you're meant to solve.

Natural Gifts

What's special about you? A gift, a talent, a way you connect—what has God given you that sets you apart? He gave it to you for a reason, and He wants you to use it to impact the world. When you do, it's no longer just a job—it's using your life to serve a greater purpose.

Experiences

What experiences have shaped you and had the most impact on your life? Think about things you've done that left a mark on you. Why was that? Reflect on past jobs, volunteer roles, or life events and then analyze what you loved about each. Look at how you served your workplace or team best, or where you felt that you were in your element. Your experiences hold clues to your purpose.

Now, connect the dots. For example, if you love baking (passion), are frustrated by the lack of local gathering spots (burden), excel at hospitality (gift), and are great at organizing events (experience), your purpose might be opening a local café or bakery where the community can come to connect.

When you dig deep and understand your purpose, you unlock the courage to pursue your dream and impact the world in a way only you can. If you can't stop thinking about the life you want, it's because you were meant to create it. That dream in your heart and mind isn't random. It's a glimpse of what's possible if you're brave enough to pursue it.

DEFINE YOUR "WHY"

Your *why* is the heartbeat of your purpose—the unshakable reason you get out of bed each morning, the fire that fuels your dreams, and the anchor that holds you steady when the road gets tough. It's not just *what* you do, but *why* you do it. It's the unique impact only you can make, the passion that drives your actions, and the vision that keeps you pushing forward. Your *why* is the key to building something that lasts.

Discovering your *why* brings clarity and authenticity to everything you do. Research backs this up: Living with a clear sense of purpose is linked to greater job satisfaction, higher income, better health, increased resilience, and even a longer life. Isn't that amazing? That's the power of knowing what drives you.

Like a personal mission statement, your *why* fuels your passion—guiding how you work, connect with others, and build a business that's about more than just profit.

As business owners, it's natural for us to tie our *why* to success and financial stability. There's nothing wrong with these aspirations. In fact, they should be a solid part of any business plan. But if we want a truly fulfilling business, our *why* must be about much more than that. As Henry Ford said, "A business that makes nothing but money is a poor business." Instead, your *why* should reflect something that can stand the test of time—

something truly fulfilling that still lights your fire a decade from now. For many, it all points back to serving others and leaving a mark.

Jessi Mason of *The Market & Mill* in Anselmo, Nebraska, lives this truth. When she and her husband returned to their hometown, they made this vow: "We'd leave Anselmo better than we found it. And we wanted to show our kids that we're proud of our town and we must give back to our town to help it." That *why*—to give back and show their kids the pride of building a thriving community—drives their every move. "If you have a reason that tugs at your heartstrings," Jessi says, "you can figure it out." Their store isn't just a business; it's a legacy, a testament to a purpose that inspires and uplifts their entire community.

Your *why* sets you apart, igniting dreams that transform not just your life but your entire community. It gives you the courage to keep going through the ups and downs of entrepreneurship—whether it's the joy of helping one client, the thrill of creating something new, or the pride and satisfaction of igniting change. It's about making a difference right where you are. So, take time to reflect. What's your *why*? And once you figure it out, let it guide you to a life and business filled with purpose, impact, and meaning.

DREAMS THAT SERVE OTHERS

When hesitation holds you back from launching your dream, it's easy to let your mind get caught in a loop of negative self-doubts: *I'm scared I'll fail. I'm stuck. I can't figure this out.* Notice the pattern? It's all about "I." But your purpose isn't just about you—it's about the lives you're called to touch.

Your thoughts shape your feelings, your feelings drive your actions, and your actions create your impact. (Read that again.)

So, if you're focused on, *I'm stuck*, *I'm scared*, or *I'm nervous*, you'll stay stuck. Because if you think you're stuck, then you'll feel frustrated and unmotivated, and you won't do anything to pursue your dream. Instead, shift your focus to serving others. How can your dream—whether it's baking cupcakes, making jewelry, or selling insurance—bring value, joy, or solutions to your community?

Your work serves a purpose. Shift your focus off of you and onto how you can transform the world around you. Is that through a business? Supporting a local group or cause? Is that through your church? If you break it down, this dream most likely serves the greater good of your community.

Maggie Haron of *Iron & Pine Design* captures this truth beautifully: "I always wanted to impact lives but didn't know how. I never imagined I could create something that would matter to someone else." Her why—to encourage others through her art—propelled her forward and opened the door to a business she never imagined. Your *why* can do the same.

Serving can also mean empowering others, not just selling a product or service. At *Branded by Rural Revival*, our rural design agency, we take a unique approach. We do the initial work in creating websites and logos and designs but we also equip clients to manage their own updates. This saves them time and money while giving them freedom they need as entrepreneurs—and genuinely serves our clients with their best interests in mind.

When you approach your dream with a heart to serve, this is what can bring true, lasting transformation to a community. Making this shift changes everything. Because your dream isn't just for you—it's about impacting others and building a legacy that outlives you. Make the people and your relationships with them the priority. Because without people, none of this matters.

THE BIGGER PICTURE

You weren't put on this earth to work your life away and quietly fade into the background. You were placed here—right in your small town—to leave a mark, to change lives, to live a story worth telling. Every choice you make, every dream you chase, makes an impact far beyond what you can see.

Rural Revival began as a podcast, but it's grown into something bigger: a platform to ignite dreamers and doers and help small businesses thrive. It's about lifting others up, sharing stories to inspire action, and building something meaningful for a purpose greater than profit. The impact has been beyond anything I imagined. Take *The Rustic Rose* in New Providence, Iowa, landing a monthly client from California after a town feature on the *Rural Revival* blog. Or *The Neighborhood Bakehouse*, whose owners moved their family to Red Oak, Iowa, and started a business after hearing Daric and Jill O'Neal's story on the podcast, convinced it was the community they'd been searching for. Then there's the collaboration between *Savannah Sevens* and *Designer's Brew* that created a western furniture collection, sparked by a connection through *Rural Revival*. Countless friendships, partnerships, and ventures have blossomed from this community, and it's an honor to provide that spark for rural America's dreamers.

What's that dream you can't let go of? That idea that keeps you up at night? Lean into it. Your small town isn't a limitation —it's your stage. Your courage to act could shift everything. It might kickstart other businesses, encourage more community revitalization, or even reshape your family's future.

Parents, think about the example you set. When your kids see you chase your dream with grit and faith, they learn it's possible for them too. You're not just building a business—you're building a legacy, showing them what it means to put faith into action and live with purpose.

This is the bigger picture: Your dream doesn't just belong to you—it belongs to your town, your people, your kids. It's a call to act, to step bravely into the unknown, and create something that lasts. In rural America, where every effort counts, your purpose can transform a community, ignite a revival, and inspire others to dream bigger.

A RIPPLE EFFECT

I'll never forget the day I was sitting in downtown Pawhuska, Oklahoma, home of Ree Drummond, *The Pioneer Woman*, taking it all in. Ree had opened a mercantile, hotel, ice cream shop, and pizza kitchen, and transformed a quiet, historic cow town into a thriving destination. When she started, vacant sidewalks and storefronts lined the streets. But her courage to build her dream drew crowds, and soon, new businesses filled those empty spaces. (If you build it, they will come, right?) As I watched that day, it hit me: So many of these business owners are living their dreams because Ree went first. Her boldness created a ripple effect, opening doors for others and reviving an entire community. Visitors, too, leave Pawhuska inspired, carrying the spark to chase their own dreams.

Your dream has that same power. It's in you for a reason, but you've got to step out. Maybe your town needs you to go first. Don't let fear or limiting beliefs hold you back. This could be the best thing you ever do—not just for you, but for everyone watching and waiting in the wings. Because when you step out, you give others permission to follow.

LIVE WITH PURPOSE, ON PURPOSE

There's never a perfect time to start. Fear will always whisper excuses to hold you back, but you've been scared long enough. You have a responsibility to live out the calling placed on your life. It's not just about you—it's about the lives you're meant to touch. Because other people—your family, your neighbors, even strangers—are counting on the breakthrough only you can bring. They're waiting for you to step into your purpose so they can find the courage to step into theirs. Who's missing out because you're not sharing your gifts? They don't need perfection; they just need you to show up with a heart to serve.

Let go of past regrets and fill your heart with hope for what's possible. God's still writing your story, and it's far from over. Take that first step, however small, and live with purpose, *on purpose*. Because when you pour your heart and soul into what you love, you light a fire that can inspire others in ways you'll never witness. That's the kind of purpose that stirs the soul.

As Henry Winkler said, "Be the most you can be. Because there are hurts to be healed, needs to be met, and if you are not the most you can be, something will remain undone forever."

★

ACTIVATION

What's your why? If you had to write a purpose statement for your life, what would it be?

Where do your passion, burden, natural gifts, and experiences intersect with a specific need in your community?

How can your purpose serve those around you? What greater impact could you make by chasing your dream?

How can you turn your passion and purpose into profit?

CHAPTER FIVE

JUST START

★

*"A ship in harbor is safe, but that is
not what ships are built for."*
— John A. Shedd

If you're ready to dip your toes into entrepreneurship, welcome to the road less traveled—the one where dreams meet courage, and the trail ahead is yours to blaze. If you're dreaming of a new venture—a business, a creative project, or a bold life change—this chapter is your wake-up call. It's time to stop waiting for the perfect moment and *just start*.

Yes, it really is that simple—and it's the top advice given by my *Rural Revival* podcast guests to aspiring entrepreneurs: *Just start*.

TAKE THE LEAP

Starting is messy, vulnerable, and exhilarating—like standing on a cliff's edge, arms wide open and heart pounding, with no guarantee of what lies below. But it's where dreams begin to take shape.

When I took the leap into entrepreneurship with *Rural Revival*, I felt both alive and unsure. It was as if I'd finally discovered a purpose I'd been searching for my whole life, yet at the same time there were a lot of unknowns. Whether editing episodes, traveling to my next speaking engagement or town visit, or answering late-night emails, I poured my heart into it— not that I had all the answers, but I gave it my best, fueled by purpose and passion. This is what starting demands of us: not perfection, but heart. As Brett McPherson of *Designer's Brew* puts it, "I just leaped. I didn't really have a plan. But it's amazing what we can do if we just try." Her words ring true. Action, not overthinking, is what brings dreams to life.

We *all* have amazing potential sitting inside of us, but potential alone doesn't create impact—action does. The best ideas, the greatest talents, or the most powerful stories mean nothing if they stay locked inside. Too many people miss their callings by staying silent—dreaming of a business but never launching, believing their vision could inspire others but refusing to speak up, longing to create spaces for connection but never inviting people to gather. The hard truth? Nobody benefits from a dream being the "best kept secret." Our dreams aren't meant to stay hidden—they're meant to change lives, starting with our own.

THERE IS NO PERFECT TIME

Let's be honest: There's no such thing as the "perfect time" to chase your dream. Life moves fast, and waiting for certainty or permission—or for all the stars to align—keeps your life on hold. Busyness and distraction can keep you stuck in survival mode and pull you away from your dreams. But dreams don't wait for ideal conditions—they grow through action and faith. If you feel unfulfilled, perhaps it's not from doing too much, but from doing too little that lights you up. Another year of unfulfilled goals isn't an option. It's time to move.

When I launched *Rural Revival*, I didn't have a clear plan—just a fire in my heart and a restless pull to do something meaningful that would bring hope to small towns. I started a podcast with no idea where it would lead, uncertain, but filled with possibility. Within weeks, I discovered a community of people who were just waiting for something like this because they needed it. They needed to know they weren't the only ones trying to bring a dream to life in a small town, to know it really was possible to live out their dreams right here in rural America. That single step changed everything. And it gave a lot of people hope to believe, *"Maybe I can do this too."*

Starting isn't about perfection; it's about showing up with purpose. Your calling wasn't meant to stay buried—it was meant to flourish. So, what's stopping you? Fear of failure? Doubt? The truth is that the only real failure is never trying.

Looking back, I didn't know the miles I'd travel, the incredible people I'd meet, or the community that would grow around *Rural Revival*. I didn't know that so many people would choose to follow this journey, each one a reminder that it's not about the numbers—it's about relationships, authenticity, and showing up as yourself. You don't need a massive following or a seamless plan to create a profitable, impactful business. You just need to start where you are, with what you have, and pour your heart into it. Your dream is waiting, and so is your community.

REAL PEOPLE, REAL COURAGE

Across rural America, dreamers and doers are proving that starting, even with uncertainty, can lead to extraordinary impact.

Their stories show that you don't need a perfect plan—just a vision and the courage to act. Take it from these *Rural Revival* podcast guests whose stories are filled with inspiration and impact:

- **Jessi Mason**, when she was a social worker with no business experience, felt an unshakable pull to bring new life to *The Market & Mill* in Anselmo, Nebraska. With no roadmap, she leaned into her vision, turning a small grocery store into a community hub that's become the heartbeat of her town. "I'm a dreamer," she says. "If it tugs at your heart strings, you can figure it out."

- **Jaime England**, when working as a physical therapist, walked into an empty building in her hometown of Manning, Iowa, and saw potential where others saw decay. Hidden under a false ceiling was stunning industrial architecture, sparking a vision she couldn't shake. "I couldn't sleep for nights," she recalls. "I was writing down every idea, picturing what it could be." That vision became *The Market Place*, a home goods store and coffee shop that now draws visitors from hours away.

- **Steffany Bettin** quit her job on a whim to open *BlueJay Boutique* in Danbury, Iowa. "I wasn't sure what it was [that I wanted to do], I just wanted a business in Danbury," she says. She decided on a boutique. Starting with a tiny storefront, Steffany trusted her instincts and built a thriving business. Now, celebrating eleven years, she's more than doubled her space and found a new purpose.

- **Grant and Jane Golliher** fought to preserve their family's *Diamond Cross Ranch* in Moran, Wyoming, where few family ranches remain. Their relentless work turned the property into a thriving tourist destination and business retreat, offering cabin stays and hosting iconic guests and celebrations against the backdrop of the Tetons. Their story is a testament to keeping a legacy alive.

- **Ryley Wimer** of *Savannah Sevens* turned isolation into an advantage with her western boutique in rural Kansas. "Living in the middle of nowhere was a blessing in disguise," she says. "It pushed me to go online instead of brick-and-mortar." Her online brand proves that small-town businesses can reach far beyond their zip codes, with or without a physical store as an option.

- **Joey and Callie Lee** brought *Osage Outfitters* to Pawhuska, Oklahoma, when it was a town with more boarded-up windows than open businesses. "Seeing those buildings with lights on again is so cool," they say. Their store sparked a transformation, bringing life and hope to a struggling downtown—soon followed by *The Pioneer Woman*'s thriving legacy of businesses.

- **Regan Doely** started *Doe A Deer*, a hand-illustrated kitchen and gift brand, as a side hustle on Facebook. She's now grown it into a full product line that's sold in shops around the world. She has also opened her flagship store in a historic building that's turning Stuart, Iowa into a destination. "You just have to take the leap at some point," she encourages. "You might not have all your ducks in a row—I definitely didn't—but I figured it out."

- **Marci Shadd** fell in love with a neglected historic hotel in Biggs, California, and knew it had to be saved. With sheer determination, she transformed *The Colonia Hotel* into a stunning wedding and event venue, becoming a photographer's muse and a community treasure.

- **Lyndsey Garber**, a western love and lifestyle photographer based in New Mexico, serves clients *beyond* her small town so she can stay rooted in her small town. "Don't limit yourself to your rural community," she says. "The internet gives us reach far beyond our hometowns, so I serve others to stay in mine." Her work shows how small-town dreamers can think globally while living locally.

- **The 72 women of** *Why Not Us* in Jefferson, Iowa, pooled their resources to revive *The Centennial*, a historic tea house that had nearly been destroyed by a massive water leak. "The goal was to return this building to life," says board member Jacque Andrew. "If we've inspired women to go for it, what more could we ask for?" adds Deb McGinn. "It's a ripple effect," Jacque replies. Today, the tea house thrives with a never-ending waitlist, proving the power of collective action.

These stories aren't about luck or perfect timing. They're about grit, trusting a vision others couldn't see, and pushing forward despite doubts. As Stacey Bannor of *Bannor Toys*—maker of beautiful, handcrafted toys that spark imagination and creativity—shares, "Had we overthought it, we wouldn't have done it. My husband bought a scroll saw, made a truck, and signed up for a church bazaar. It unraveled into something great." Each of these entrepreneurs faced uncertainty, naysayers, and obstacles, but they started anyway—and their communities are better because of it.

WHY WE HESITATE (AND HOW TO PUSH THROUGH)

Starting is hard because fear is loud. It whispers doubts, replays past failures, and convinces us to wait for the "right" moment. But waiting for certainty is a trap, especially in places like rural America, where familiarity feels safe.

I get it—chasing a dream feels like a gamble. But here's the thing: Fear robs people of potential, keeping them stuck in jobs they hate or lives that feel average because they're too scared to take a chance. We miss out on so much of what could be in rural America because too many are afraid to take the risk required to chase their dreams, when they could be chasing something extraordinary. The real risk isn't failure—it's never trying. So, we each must determine which is scarier: trying and failing or never knowing what could have been.

Michelle Hamilton of *Dandelion Naturals* in Hayfield, Minnesota, faced that fear head-on. "It's scary," she admits, "but if you don't do it, you'll never know if you can succeed."

Many of us wait for the perfect timing, the perfect plan, or the perfect skills. But perfection is an illusion. Jessi Mason had no business experience, Jaime England and Ryley Wimer had no retail experience, yet they figured it out by starting small and learning as they went. Learn to embrace the messiness of starting—because this is where growth happens and where character is built. It's a foundation you can't build any other way.

Not everyone will understand your vision, and that's okay. Many of these entrepreneurs faced skeptics, but they chose to trust their instincts and built something extraordinary. Surround yourself with cheerleaders who believe in your dream. Tune out the negative voices. I've learned that you don't owe doubters an explanation—just action. As Lettie McKinney, who returned home to take over her family's *MC- Ranch* in southwest Kansas, puts it, "Just start. If you have a dream in your heart, do it. You'll learn as you go, and people respect that courage. It's so rewarding." Her words remind us that bravery isn't the absence of fear—it's moving forward despite it.

DO IT SCARED

Fear will always try to hold you back, whispering doubts and worst-case scenarios. But waiting to feel fearless is a trap. My best advice? *Do it scared.* Entrepreneurship demands you step outside your comfort zone and will force you to grow, in the most beautiful and challenging ways. But this is what the journey's all about. This is where it all pays off. Lean into those hard times. It's not about pretending you have it all figured out —it's about trusting the calling inside you.

When Katie Adams left a stable job to launch *Stuart Flowers & Gifts*, she asked herself a powerful question: *What would you do if you could not fail?* That simple shift in perspective unlocked her courage. Similarly, Lynne Thomas of *Barnstorm Coffee* listened to the persistent nudge of an idea that wouldn't let go. "If an idea keeps coming back to you, there's a reason," she said. That reason goes back to your purpose. It's the whisper in your heart saying, *This is what you're meant to do.*

Keith and Sandi Mitcham of *Mitcham Livestock* bravely uprooted their lives from Georgia to Cherokee, Oklahoma, to revive a neglected feedlot they discovered through a fortuitous Google search. Escaping the urban sprawl of metro Atlanta, where subdivisions and a movie studio displaced their rural roots, they poured their life savings into building a custom cattle feeding operation from scratch. Despite some initial financing hurdles and the emotional weight of leaving their roots, their faith and resilience guided them through. "My prayer was, 'Dear Lord, just close doors that no man can open and open doors that no man can close,'" Sandi reflects. Keith echoes, "If you're in God's will and you've got that dream, it'll come together." Their risk has paid off, and they've flourished in their new community, where neighbors have showed up to support their vision. "I love my life here," Sandi says. "I still drive down the road and say, 'I can't believe I live here.'"

Being passionate and pouring your whole heart into everything you do can be a blessing and a burden. When something goes wrong, your heart can break in ways you didn't know possible. But when things fall into place, it fills your soul beyond anything you ever imagined. You get to work to build something meaningful, forge connections with extraordinary people, and wake up each day driven by a mission that's uniquely yours. Every unsteady step, every late-night doubt, every small win builds something bigger than you could've planned. As Steve Jobs said, "The people who are crazy enough to think they can change the world are the ones who do."

Stepping into the unknown is uncomfortable, even terrifying, but that is where transformation begins. Pursue your dreams despite the fear. Be brave enough to go for it anyway—because your dream is a call to change lives, starting with your own. And this is exactly what our small towns need.

START SMALL, DREAM BIG

A small beginning is a catalyst. It ignites the potential for something extraordinary for people like us—the trailblazers, creatives, and dreamers—who dare to challenge the status quo and believe for something different in our small towns. We don't need a million-dollar budget or a flawless business plan to begin. Many iconic brands started simple—with one product, no roadmap, and a lot of heart.

For Paige Ehnle Heaton of *No Roots Boots*, it was an Airstream travel trailer named Pearl and a vision of a mobile boot shop, filled with the best boots she could find or dream up. It was a wild idea, but it was hers, and she couldn't ignore it. "When I started *No Roots Boots*, I was overwhelmed. The logistics of running a mobile business, the endless decisions, the fear of failure—it was a lot. Even with all my passion, there were days I questioned myself. But I kept going, one foot in front of the other. I learned how to back up the Airstream (badly at first). I figured out what products resonated with my customers. I stumbled, adapted, and grew. Each challenge was a building block, shaping me into the business owner I am today."

Marcy Bergman shared a similar sentiment about her own start with her *Fueled by Faith* coffee shop. "We popped up about six times, and I felt really silly every time we opened it—just vulnerable, like, does everybody think this is a dumb idea?" But people kept coming. That's the wonder of starting—you don't have to have it all figured out. You just have to show up, even when it feels awkward or scary. The right people will find you.

Laura Capp described how her bookstore and stationery shop, *Postscript*, has allowed her to flourish. "It's truly allowed me to step into the dream version of myself that I carry around in my head." That's what starting does—it bridges the gap between who you are and who you're meant to be.

The most sustainable businesses are built little by little, consistently over time. As you begin something significant, don't underestimate the power of small beginnings. Take that first step, even if it's small.

- **Begin with One Idea:** *Bannor Toys* started with a single wooden truck. I started with a podcast. Focus on one product or service and make it the best it can be. Quality over quantity builds a foundation for growth.

- **Listen to Your Customers:** Stay connected to your audience and let their needs guide you. Regan Doely's success came from listening and adapting, proving that customer feedback is a roadmap for growth.

- **Grow Intentionally:** Fast growth can be fleeting, but steady progress builds something lasting. Jessi Mason didn't aim for overnight success—she focused on reviving one business, and the ripple effect is transforming her community.

- **Leverage Your Resources:** Ryley Wimer used the internet to reach beyond her small town, showing that tools like a website and social media can amplify your impact. Start with what you have—your skills, your passion, your community.

Success isn't about getting in at the "right time." It's about digging in when the bank says, "Your business model doesn't fit." It's making sacrifices now that will allow you to support a long-term dream. It's hearing "no" and letting it fuel your path.

As Marci Shadd's hotel revival shows, one bold step can preserve history and inspire others.

Start with one product, one service, one idea. Stay connected to your customers and listen to their needs, as Shanna Lindberg of *Soul Sister Ceramics* in Courtland, Kansas, did. "Starting small and growing as you go was my biggest asset—listening to what people need, starting slow, and building upon that," she says. Growth doesn't have to be fast—it just has to be intentional. Focus on your *why*, not just the bottom line. As *Why Not Us* member Deb McGinn says, "It's a ripple effect." Don't underestimate it. One small step can spark a movement.

TRUST THE PROCESS

As you start to step out, hold your plans loosely. Keep your heart open, listen to your customers, and trust the process. Your goal is long-term success, not a short-lived trend. As the Gollihers' ranch shows, relentless commitment to a vision can create a legacy that outlives you.

My best advice?

- **Ignore the doubters.** Not everyone will understand your vision, and that's okay. Don't waste energy justifying yourself. As I learned early on, you don't need to explain yourself to the doubters, the naysayers, or the "yeah, but" folks. Surround yourself with supporters who see your potential, cheer you on, and believe in your dream.

- **Hold your dreams close.** Protect your vision early— nurture it quietly until it's ready to shine. Sometimes, sharing too soon can put water on your fire. Let those dreams grow in your heart until they're strong enough to stand on their own.

- **Test it out.** Marcy Bergman opened her *Fueled by Faith* coffee trailer on Saturday mornings in Sumner, Iowa, to gauge interest. It worked. Now she runs her business from a cute downtown space, balancing it with her bank job. But she may have never gotten to that point had she not tried it out with the trailer first.

- **Commit to the journey.** I love the advice Cassie Everson of *Wanderlust Skulls* gave on the podcast. "Patience and never giving up is so important to your journey. The right people will always find you." When you chase what sets your soul on fire, the path begins to unfold, one unsure step at a time. Trust the process—it's a marathon, not a sprint.

As Michelle Myers said, "I think the fear of failing and the fear of other people judging you is the biggest stopping point for a lot of people. So, getting out of your own head and your own way and just realizing that those things don't really matter—and if you fail, at least you tried."

Bottom line: Your dream is worth the risk.

PRACTICAL STEPS TO START TODAY

Ready to take that first step? Here's how to begin, no matter where you are:

- **Clarify Your Why:** Remind yourself of your *why* statement from chapter 4 and write down why this dream matters to you. Is it to serve your community, like Jessi Mason? To preserve history, like Marci Shadd? Your *why* will anchor you through uncertainty.

- **Take One Action:** Start with something small—buy a domain name, sketch a logo, or reach out to a potential mentor. Andrea Stordahl of *Minnesota Rust* started by opening a store in a struggling town, and that single choice sparked a revival.

- **Learn As You Go:** You don't need to know everything. Starting is about trusting the journey. Jaime England of *The Market Place* learned by doing—researching and writing down ideas. As Jessi Mason of *The Market & Mill* says, "Everything's figure-out-able." From YouTube to mentors to fellow entrepreneurs, answers are out there if you're willing to search them out.

- **Find Your Tribe:** No dream thrives in isolation. Build a support system and surround yourself with people who believe in you, like the *Why Not Us* women who leaned on each other. Join a community—online or local—to cheer you on. The *Rural Revival* community is a great place to find encouragement and accountability!

- **Push Past the Roadblocks:** Roadblocks are inevitable, but they're not dead ends. Here's how to push through common hurdles:

  - **Decision Fatigue:** Entrepreneurship is a series of choices, and indecision can paralyze you. Stop waiting for more information or assurance—it won't come. Make a decision, learn from it, and keep moving.

- **Distractions:** Social media, Netflix, or a packed schedule can steal your focus. Ask yourself, *Does this support the life I'm trying to create?* Cut out what doesn't serve your dream, even temporarily, to make space for what matters.

- **Fear of Failure:** Failure isn't the opposite of success; it's part of it. Jill Winger of *The Prairie Homestead* says, "You can't let failure stop you." Every misstep teaches you something. Faith, not fear, drives progress.

Don't overthink it. As Stacey Bannor's story proves, a single step—like signing up for a church bazaar—can unravel into something great. The key is to act, even if it's imperfectly. Tia Berens of *The Barn at Aspen Acres* shares her own wisdom. "Go for it. But also know it's gonna be hard. You have to have the tenacity and the grit to be able to have all those moments of 'no's' to get through it."

STOP PLAYING IT SAFE

I know that voice in your head, the one whispering, *What if you crash and burn?* It's loud, isn't it? But waiting until you feel totally fearless to make a move? That'll keep you stuck, and you'll wait forever. The real risk is never trying.

If you're an entrepreneur, I've got good news: You're wired for risk. This means you've already got that spark, that willingness to take a leap. So why let fear call the shots? Sure, things might not work out. But what if they do? What if your idea turns into something bigger than you ever imagined? That's not just daydreaming—that's faith. Faith isn't about having it all figured out or pretending everything's fine. It's looking at how God has shown up in your life before and trusting He'll do it again. It's taking that scary step, knowing growth is waiting on the other side.

Entrepreneurship is messy. There's no perfect roadmap. But every small business you see today started with someone who said, "I'm going for it," despite the fear. God gave you gifts— your skills, passions, and ideas—and He expects you to use them, not bury them in doubt.

Take Josh Smith of *Montana Knife Company*, who spent twenty years envisioning his dream business. "People see a brand like ours explode and it seems like it's overnight, but it's been brewing in my head since I was nineteen years old. I registered this name with the state of Montana when I was nineteen, but I didn't launch it until I was thirty-nine." He planned and visualized what MKC could become, but it wasn't until he took action that his vision came to life. So, he quit his job as a lineman and went all in. As Josh put it, "At some point, the dream has to become reality. Go get it!" Now every knife launch sells out within minutes, and the company keeps outgrowing its space as inventory demands surge.

Big dreams—God-sized dreams—feel overwhelming because they're meant to. They're bigger than you, and that's where faith kicks in. God doesn't call you to what's easy. He calls you to what requires Him to step in and do what only He can do—make the impossible happen. His plan for you is bigger than your fears. Let your life be a story only He could write.

Stop letting fear shrink your vision. Stop playing out worst-case scenarios like a bad movie in your head. You weren't made for a small, safe life. Faith doesn't mean you have all the answers—it just means you show up. Take the step. Speak up. Trust God. You don't fail by trying—you fail by staying stuck.

FIND YOUR SWEET SPOT

When you chase your dream with courage, you unlock a door to something extraordinary: you find your *sweet spot*. It's that moment when you wake up and everything clicks—your heart is steady, your soul is on fire, and your vision is clear. You're at peace with where you've been, what you've overcome, and where you're going. It's not a destination you plotted on a map or planned in advance. It's a state of being, where all your efforts start to pay off, and your work feels like a calling.

Josh and Sarah Holmquist of *Normal Roasting Company* in Burwell, Nebraska, discovered this when they added a coffee shop to their roasting business. It seemed like a natural next step. But it didn't take long for them to realize wholesale is their sweet spot. "Wholesale is the backbone of our business and honestly where I think we have the most fun," says Sara. They have since shifted their focus back to wholesale and are all the happier for it.

For me, the sweet spot came into focus on those long drives home after an interview or event, as I cruised down the road, soaking in the moment. It was there I realized this unexpected dream had opened the door to a creative canvas—a life where my passion spills out every single day, where work feels more like play. *Rural Revival* interrupted my life in a way I never could've scripted until it stared me in the face. My dream wasn't always pretty or polished—definitely more chaotic than clear at the start—but I kept going. I persisted.

This book is my thank you to the journey that has shaped me into who I am today. But more than that, it's a call for you: *If you have a dream, chase it with everything you've got.* The sweet spot isn't something you stumble upon by accident. It's found through courage, trust, and a relentless pursuit of what sets your soul on fire.

YOUR DREAM IS WAITING

This is my challenge to you: *just start*. Right now, right where you are. Dream big but start small. Don't worry about having it all figured out. Don't let what other people may think hold you back. If a dream is on your heart, it's there for a reason, calling you to step out—and into your best life.

Picture your dream life. What does it look like? How does it feel? Work backward from there, one step at a time. Embrace that there will be hard days, lonely days, and days when you question everything. But those low moments make the highs so much sweeter—because there will also be days when your heart wants to burst because you're right smack dab in the middle of living out your dream. As I've learned, there's pure joy in work that lights your soul on fire—work that's more than a paycheck, work that leaves a legacy.

You don't need to feel ready. You just need to feel the dream pulling you forward. Your journey doesn't have to be like anyone else's. You only have to begin. Because when you begin, you become someone new, someone who decided that your dream was worth showing up for. Even when it was hard. One day, you'll look back and realize that taking your first step was the moment it all began. And you'll be so proud you didn't give up on yourself.

This book is for the dreamers in small places—kitchen tables, garages, tractor cabs, basement warehouses, small dots on the map. It's for the ones who don't fit the mold, who dare to pave their own path. It's for you, standing at the edge of your own cliff, heart pounding, ready to jump.

Take the leap. Do it scared. Bet on yourself. The life you dream of is closer than you think. And your small town is your stage, ready and waiting for your leap.

Join our Rural Revival community at ruralrevival.co/community.

★

ACTIVATION

What's the next right step for your dream?

What fear is holding you back from starting, and how can you reframe it as an opportunity for growth?

Who can you turn to for support or encouragement as you take your first step?

What would you do if you knew you couldn't fail?

CHAPTER SIX

BUILD A BUSINESS YOU LOVE

★

"Your work is going to fill a large part of your life, and the only way to be truly satisfied is to do what you believe is great work. And the only way to do great work is to love what you do."
— Steve Jobs

In a world that pushes for bigger and better and faster, set those expectations aside and ask yourself: *When it comes to my dream, what do I want success to look like?*

Building a business you love starts with setting goals rooted in purpose *and* profit. It's about creating something lasting that reflects your heart, serves your small town, *and* allows you to make a living. What strategies can you incorporate in your business to build something that you love, that can last?

As we've been exploring, business is so much more than transactions. It's about the people, places, and memories made along the way. So, let's make sure you're building a business that feels like home—one that prioritizes people, connection, and joy over chasing what the world would tell you to do.

If I could put together a list of things I believe can make the biggest difference in how you approach your dream and your business, and some of the hangups that can creep in along the way, this chapter is it.

REDEFINE SUCCESS

The road to success is rarely a straight line—it's more like a winding, dusty trail full of detours, breakdowns, and moments that make you question everything. The sooner you accept this truth, the sooner you will realize this is just part of the journey—not for you only, but for everyone on this entrepreneurial adventure.

As any good business coach will tell you, traditional goals such as growing followers or hitting sales targets matter. But don't stop there; dig deeper. How can your business impact lives? Brighten someone's day? Strengthen your town? As my friend Robin Lunsford, a retail veteran who co-leads some of our Dream Builder trainings, says, "Sometimes you just have to listen to someone tell you about their cat's surgery, because that's what's important to them." What if success meant focusing on meaningful conversations over Instagram likes? Or drawing in visitors to boost local shops?

"Rather than focusing on our numbers on social media, we really focused on the people," says Jasmin Stidham of *Stidham Outfitters*. "We built so many amazing relationships that the following kind of came more naturally." Purpose-driven goals—such as fostering connection or collaborating with other businesses—create impact that outlasts profit.

Redefining success also means having the courage to pivot. For seasoned entrepreneurs, it might mean abandoning paths that no longer fit, setting boundaries and standing up for yourself even when it's hard, or reworking what you've built. It's having the grit to pour your heart and soul into late nights, the grace to admit when you're wrong, and the resolve to keep going when skeptics say, "That'll never work."

Long-lasting rural businesses thrive because they're about more than transactions; they're also about impact. "Being part of the Main Street family, I've built friendships and customer relationships that are the most rewarding part," says Liz Feldkamp of *Liz's Bridal* in Seneca, Kansas. When people engage with a small business, they're not interacting with a faceless machine, they're connecting with you—a real person who's poured their heart and soul into every detail. That's what sets you apart—not chasing a corporate ladder, but climbing mountains your own way, building something that's about community over profit. And trust me, the results come when you lead with heart.

In small towns, where service is in our DNA, these goals ensure your business endures while making a difference that resonates far beyond the bottom line. "Don't worry about *how* you're successful," says Matt Floyd of *Matt's Bat*. "Focus on helping others, and you'll become invaluable to your community." When you lead with purpose, doing what's right for your people, the rest will follow. Word-of-mouth spreads when you prioritize impact, creating a ripple effect of loyalty and growth. Focus on serving, not selling, and your business becomes a beacon in your town, drawing people who believe in your vision as much as you do.

BUILD A BUSINESS AROUND YOUR LIFE (NOT THE OTHER WAY AROUND)

Entrepreneurship offers a special gift: the freedom to design a business that fits *you*. In small towns, this flexibility is not just possible—it's celebrated. Closing early so you can go coach your kid's ball team? Got it. Only open on weekends because that's all your schedule allows? We're cool with that. Only open one weekend a month? We can make that work, too. This approach might not work in a big city, but it works in a small town because these are the things our lives revolve around. Small town customers get it. They value authenticity over availability.

Marcy Bergman's nontraditional format with *Fueled by Faith*, where she is open only on Saturdays, is a perfect example. "The coffee shop has given people the encouragement that it doesn't have to be a full-time gig, it doesn't have to be every day. If you have another job and you're passionate about this, it can be once a week. And if that's all you have to give to the community, that's great. Whatever it looks like for you, you can try it and you don't have to be the status quo of 8-5, Monday through Friday. You can make it whatever you want, and I think your community will support it."

When businesses try to be all things to all people, or evolve into something they didn't want to be, business owners wear themselves out to the point it's no longer fun for them. Every. Single. Time. Making changes to your business, especially one that has grown into something people really love (even if you don't love it), can be hard. But sometimes you have to reset and go back to what works for you.

That's what Seth and Jasmin Stidham, of *Stidham Outfitters* (now *Stidham Saddlery*) in Johnson City, Texas, did. Their store was thriving, but it had snowballed into something that no longer sparked joy. They made the brave choice to pivot, refocusing on their passion for custom leather goods and craftsmanship. "This change was about recognizing the business wasn't our passion anymore," Jasmin says. "It was performing well, but were we in love with it?"

Lots of people will have opinions about what they think your business should be, but they're not you. At the end of the day, you must do what fits and works for you. Don't let others' expectations define your business. You weren't meant to fit into someone else's mold, to shrink, or to conform to their comfort. You were born to expand, create, and carve out your own space —in a way that fits *your* dream. Build a business that feels like home. Not the one that looks good on paper. Not that one that makes everyone else happy. Build a business that is yours. Because the last thing you want is to feel trapped in your business.

SLOW GROWTH OFTEN MEANS GOOD GROWTH

Contrary to what our fast-paced world may tell you, in life and business, you are often rewarded for going slow, one step at a time, and doing small things right. People tend to lose because they want things fast, but it's usually the slow, intentional steps that build the strongest foundations.

Everyone loves the highlight reel on social media. We're all guilty of using this as a barometer or standard for our own businesses. But what we don't see are the late nights, the failures, or the blood, sweat, tears, and prayers it took to get there. As Dave Ramsey puts it, "There's no such thing as an overnight success, just years of grit no one saw." It's hearing "no" repeatedly, only to find the right "yes" later. It's investing in an online presence that doesn't yet yield orders or showing up at events where sales are slim, but exposure builds your name. These trials shape not only your business, but your character.

Don't chase the myth of overnight success or feel like a failure when progress takes time. Be a student of your business, honing your skills with each step. Surround yourself with mentors and "business besties" who challenge and inspire you, sharpening you like iron. Experiment boldly, keep what works, and learn from what doesn't. Celebrate small wins—a new skill, a meaningful customer connection—as each is a brick in your foundation. "When you start a business, it seems like this giant mountain to climb," says Lindsy Trotter of *Chilled* freezer meals. "But you just have to keep doing the next right thing."

If you want to grow, it sometimes means going slow, being intentional, doing things others are too busy to do, and creating a community instead of just selling. As Maartje Murphy of *Cows & Co. Creamery* in Carrington, North Dakota shared, "For the first two years we worked probably every single weekend to get our name out there. I said yes to basically anyone who would hire me or want to have gelato. We sacrificed a lot, but I wouldn't want it any other way." Continue to trust your vision and put in the work. Count every blessing, roadblock, and incredible person you have met along the way. Because slow growth, rooted in purpose and resilience, builds a foundation that lasts.

AUTHENTICITY IS YOUR SUPERPOWER

In a world obsessed with social media likes and followers, it's easy to focus on metrics and lose sight of what matters. But there's a superpower far greater than any social media strategy. That superpower is authenticity. No one can do *you* better than you. When you lean into what makes your business unique—

your story, your values, your vision—you build a business that stands out by being unmistakably yours.

For me, staying authentic meant building a business that felt true to who I am—and true to who my audience is. *Rural Revival* isn't about me—it's about storytelling, connection, and celebrating *you*—the dreamers and doers of rural America. It's about sharing stories and products made by people I've met along this wild journey. It's about finding ways to help you thrive right where you are. It's about saying no to things that don't align with my values so I can say yes to what does.

I've learned to stay in my lane, to let my unique style and personality shine through. That's the secret sauce—not chasing trends or trying to be someone else, but leaning into what makes you, *you*. When you do that, you have no competition. No one else has your original ideas. No one else has your grit and your passion. No one else has your vision for your dream. So don't let comparison steal your joy. Keep your head down, stay true to your vision, and continue to chase your dreams with everything you've got.

BUILD A BRAND THAT IMPACTS

A strong brand doesn't sell; it invites people into your vision. When people buy, they don't just buy your product, they buy into all you stand for. So instead of marketing a product, build a vision people want to be a part of. Here's how to create a brand that draws them in:

- **Root Your Brand in Purpose:** What's the deeper mission behind what you do? Why does it matter? When your audience sees the heart behind your brand, they'll feel like they're part of something bigger.

- **Share Your Values:** People connect with brands that align with their beliefs. What do you stand for? What do you refuse to compromise on? Your values create a sense of belonging.

- **Paint a Picture:** Show your audience where your brand is going and how they can be part of the journey. Whether it's freedom, empowerment, transformation, or growth—help them see the future they can create with you.

- **Make Your Brand About Them:** Your vision should invite your audience to step into their next level. Show them how your brand fits into their lives. They should feel like being part of your brand helps them become the person they want to be.

A brand built on purpose and authenticity doesn't just sell—it leads. It turns customers into a community that believes in your dream as much as you do. When you build a brand that's true to you, it attracts people who already feel like friends.

BIGGER IS NOT ALWAYS BETTER

The dream in your heart is about more than just outcomes—it's about connection and purpose. The pressure to scale up—grow faster, get bigger, do more—is relentless, whispering doubts such as *Why not scale up?* or *Why not take on more?* But bigger isn't always better—it's often just more. If growth means managing endless tasks, disconnected from the people who make your work meaningful, is it worth it?

Consider a small-town general store owner. Stocking every product under the sun doesn't guarantee more profit or loyalty—it just means a bigger inventory. The same concept applies to your business. Scaling up can dilute your impact if it pulls you away from your purpose.

For me, success lies in knowing your stories, seeing how my work inspires your dreams, and helping you thrive in what you're called to do. And I have to work hard to make sure that stays front and center. That's why I resist the frenzy of "more" and focus on what matters—personal touches, authentic connections, and a business that feels like home. I'm still the one who answers messages and emails, creates content, and dreams up ways to serve my community, even if it's messy and imperfect.

So, stay intentional. Build a business that reflects your values and serves your community, not one that chases "more" for its own sake. Your customers feel the difference when your heart is in it—and that's what keeps them coming back.

FAIL FORWARD AND EMBRACE THE SEASONS

As an entrepreneur, you'll face seasons of uncertainty—those in-between moments when you're unsure of the next step or where you'll be in five years. I think a lot of dreamers struggle to find purpose in the here and now because they love to look forward, plan for growth, and dream bigger. But the gold often lies in taking in the moment and finding purpose right where you are, even while you're working on those goals to get you where you want to be.

You will fail at times; that's inevitable. But the key is to learn from those failures and keep moving forward. Here's a secret: You've got to fail to grow. Those tough days, those let-downs, those ideas that crash and burn—they're not the end. They're the beginning of something new. I've made my fair share of mistakes, but each one taught me something. It pushed me to try again, to think differently, to keep chasing the purpose that's woven into my heart.

I learned this early on, as people emailed me to ask for help with their small businesses and small towns, but I wasn't quite sure how to answer. After all, I was just called to start a podcast, right? But every pivot, every trial and error, led me to where I am today. *Rural Revival* is the story of a dream built from grit, grace, and a whole lot of heart—a journey that's about people, purpose, and showing rural America what's possible.

As Justin Slack of *The Post & Office* said, "We don't look at things as failures. If it doesn't work, we'll try something else. But we learn something from it." Lynne Thomas of *Barnstorm Coffee* offers a similar perspective. "I don't look at a lot of these things as failures, a lot of them are just learning experiences, and you just have to keep picking up and moving forward."

The most successful entrepreneurs are often the same people who fail the most—because they're the ones who *try* the most. "When you find failure, be thankful for it," says Jason Smith of *Dream Dirt* auction company. Show up, even when it's messy, and trust that every setback is a setup for a comeback.

If you've made bad decisions in the past, please forgive yourself. You did the best you could with the information you had at the time. Today you would probably handle the situation differently. But don't let that hold you back from never taking a risk again. Successful entrepreneurs aren't those who never fail —they're the ones who keep trying. And when life knocks you down and gives you lemons, pick yourself back up, embrace the season, and make lemonade.

Life, like any meaningful pursuit, moves in seasons, and each season serves a purpose. Looking back, I see how these seasons have played out in my life—seasons of struggle, celebration, growth, and fine-tuning. But in every one, I must slow down and remind myself that *This is what I do for a living. And I wouldn't change it for a thing.*

You don't have to love every season of life, but don't overlook them either. God weaves purpose into every moment, no matter the circumstances. So slow down, take in the moments, and find purpose right where your feet are planted. Trust God's timing as you keep chasing your dreams with a big heart and open mind—because the future holds possibilities you can't yet imagine.

AVOID BURNOUT, EMBRACE REST, AND REIGNITE CREATIVITY

Burnout sneaks up fast when you're a small-town entrepreneur juggling every role—designer, marketer, photographer, shipper, janitor, customer service expert, and more. The hustle is real, and no matter how much you love what you do, managing all these things can be exhausting. Anyone with me?

In small towns, we're blessed with wide-open spaces to breathe, no matter how crazy life gets. Yet when someone asks, "How's work? How's life?" we often default to one word: *busy.* It's a badge we wear, as if constant hustle equals success. Yet running in all these directions steals time, intention, and joy. And we before we know it, we're too busy to connect, too busy to create, too busy to live.

For a farmer, harvest season comes and goes. There's a time to put in all the hard work and long hours to bring in the crop, but then harvest is over, and the pace slows for a while. Many of us have roots in the farming way of life, the work ethic it instilled, and the family ties that run deep. And as small business owners, we love what we're doing as much as those farmers love farming. It's what makes us come alive. But if we're not careful, we can start operating our businesses in a perpetual "harvest season." We get so busy building a business that we forget to live.

Have you ever noticed that clarity comes when life slows down? In those moments, we reconnect with what truly matters —checking in on loved ones, supporting local businesses, and cherishing time together. Creativity starts to flow again. And it's in these quieter moments we can learn that being busy isn't an excuse to forget about what matters.

Remember that rest is just as important as the work. Part of the freedom of being an entrepreneur is that you get to set your own pace. Taking time to rest can recharge your batteries, fuel your creativity, and inspire your best work. And pausing to soak it all in—this is living. In the middle of the chaos, challenges, wins, and setbacks, this is where you're meant to be, doing exactly what you're meant to do. So don't forget to slow down, be grateful, and cherish the moments you once prayed for. Instead of being busy all the time, make time to rest and recharge. Your business thrives when you do, so find that balance and keep pushing forward with unwavering purpose.

DON'T QUIT. HAVE FUN. ENJOY THE JOURNEY.

Starting a business is tough. You'll sacrifice money, sleep, and time, and it might take over your life. But a 9-to-5 grind isn't any easier if you're underpaid, overlooked, uninspired, and stuck with bosses you can't stand. Life can be hard either way, so choose your hard—the one that lights you up.

As an entrepreneur, the journey to success isn't just a path, it's an ongoing adventure packed with challenges at every turn. What sets extraordinary entrepreneurs apart? Their relentless grit, unshakable belief in their vision, and their refusal to quit. You start from nothing—zero experience, zero customers—and push forward with faith, discipline, and sheer determination. But the secret is knowing success is not just about the grind, it's about finding joy in the process.

"I firmly believe business done right should be fun," says Paige Ehnle Heaton of *No Roots Boots*. "If it's not, step back and reconnect with why you started." Too often we look at where we need to be instead of seeing just how far we've come. Every win, big or small, is proof of our courage, resilience, and vision.

Grant Golliher of *Diamond Cross Ranch*, says, "Success is not how much money you make or how fancy of house you've got or what kind of car you drive, it's are you happy? Do you have a reason to get up every morning? Do you have a purpose?" His wife, Jane, agrees. "To me success is being happy with what you do."

If you chase goals but forget to live, you miss the point. Research backs this up: It's not hitting targets that fulfills you most—it's the growth. The journey of stretching yourself is more rewarding than any finish line. You don't need to wait for the business to launch, the building to be finished, or the big break to arrive. Find joy today. The to-do list will always be there. Savor the life you're building now and celebrate the messy, beautiful journey. Because you're not just building a business—you're building a legacy. And that's worth showing up for every single day.

THE PATH FORWARD

Sometimes success looks nothing like you thought it would. It's not about luck—it's the result of hard work, sacrifice, and a stubborn refusal to quit. It's betting on yourself when nobody else does, showing up raw and real, even when fear and doubt creep in. It's knowing that the life you dream of might be on the other side of some big sacrifices. It's breaking free from the box that wants to keep you small.

Building a business you love demands courage and relentless commitment. It may require you to stand up for yourself when it's uncomfortable, walk away from jobs that don't fit your purpose, and chase wild dreams even when others don't believe in you. It requires focus, discipline, grit, and perseverance.

You might work countless nights and weekends, lose friends who don't get your vision, or have to pick yourself up and repeatedly try again. You might need to swallow your pride, accept tough feedback, and find the courage to pivot when necessary. You'll learn to lean into the chaos, arms wide open. You'll need to make sure purpose and impact don't get overshadowed by profit alone. And sometimes, you'll overcomplicate things and need a reminder of why you began.

But when you find your rhythm, you run with it. "Never quitting is literally going to change your life if you stick with it," says Cassie Everson. "That attitude is going to get you a lot farther than talent ever could." Success isn't defined by crossing a finish line—it's the wild pursuit of a purpose that burns in your heart, through all the ups and downs. Every struggle, every step, becomes worth it.

So, here's to chasing your dreams with passion, learning to fail forward, and embracing every moment—the highs, the lows, and the beautiful chaos in between. Build a business that's truly yours, grounded in purpose, and keep going until it feels like home. Because anything worth doing is hard, and this? This is worth everything.

★

ACTIVATION

How do you currently measure success in your business?

What part of your business brings you the most joy? How can you structure your work to prioritize these tasks, even if it means saying no to others' expectations?

What season are you in right now? What's one action you can take to embrace this season's purpose, even if it's challenging?

Where can you find contentment in the here and now while still chasing your dreams?

CHAPTER SEVEN

THE POWER OF COMMUNITY

★

*"It's one thing to have a dream, it's another
when others believe in it too."*
— *Joanna Gaines*

More than the wide-open spaces, more than a name on a water tower, it's the people that are the heartbeat of our small towns. In rural America, community pride isn't just about the place—it's about the stories, values, and faces that shape our lives. It's the neighbor who waves from the porch, the local diner where everyone knows your order, and the Friday night football game where the whole town shows up in school colors to cheer on the home team. This is the bond that weaves us together, the charm that transforms our towns into living, breathing communities, far more than just dots on a map.

My journey with *Rural Revival* has taught me one undeniable truth: A dream is only as strong as the people who help it grow. This isn't just my story—it's *ours*—the dreamers, doers, and believers who make it real. It's the small business owners pouring their hearts into their craft, the people showing up to our events with infectious enthusiasm, the friends who cheer us on when doubt creeps in, and the family who helps us plant roots back home. Without all of this, my dream would still be a scrapbook of ideas on a vision board. Together, we're breathing life into rural America—one connection, one story, one dream at a time.

THE DREAMERS AND DOERS

Life is a wild, winding road, and who you choose to travel it with can make all the difference. Take my friend Joni Nash. From the day I came to Pawhuska, Oklahoma, to interview her, she's welcomed me into her world, believed in my wildest dreams, and lived with a fierce, generous spirit. She's often raised her hand to hit the road with me for podcast interviews. She's a reminder that the right people don't just cheer you on— they jump right in with you and propel you forward.

I'm endlessly inspired by the resilient, purposeful people I've met on this journey. These dreamers and doers live unapologetically, their authenticity and tenacity lifting everyone around them. They're not just a support system—they're catalysts, helping to turn doubts into drive and ideas into reality.

These are your people who will bring out the very best in you —passionate, intentional, challenging, encouraging people—real people. The ones who drown your doubts, fuel your ambitions, and walk with you through the messy, beautiful chaos. The ones who make you feel alive, who remind you that your dreams aren't crazy, and cheer you on every step of the way. With your people by your side, you're not just surviving the journey— you're rewriting what's possible.

COMMUNITY OVER COMPETITION

I've noticed a new movement stirring in rural America, rewriting the rules of what it means to win. It's not about clawing your way to the top or outshining your neighbor. It's about lifting each other up, cheering each other on, and realizing that when you're your authentic self, you have no competition—because when everyone is uniquely themselves, everyone has something special to offer to the world. "There's room at the table for everybody," says Brandi Lahey of *The Tipsy Farmer*, capturing the heart of this shift. This mindset is a game-changer, turning "me" into "we" and sparking a shift that's unstoppable.

Community over competition isn't just a catchphrase—it's becoming a way of life. As my podcast guests often say, "A rising tide lifts all ships." Imagine a world where people support people—where we're not sizing each other up, but instead rooting for each other's dreams. It's a road less traveled, and it's not always easy. But it's one worth taking.

The movers and shakers I feature on my podcast—the ones who give it all they've got and bring hope to their small towns—share a common thread. They choose to put community over competition. It's more than just a business strategy, it's a lifestyle. And as they embrace it, it opens a whole new world to not only them, but the community around them, and it makes everybody shine.

When Andrea Stordahl of *Minnesota Rust* started to revitalize her town, the idea of community over competition was at the forefront of her vision. "Let's bring in people who complement each other, don't compete against each other, have similar clients, but they all bring something new to the table. We wanted to make it this community business that was all about working together—which I think used to be the model everywhere." It's worked, and the town is thriving. "Now I'm surrounded by people with the same kind of mindset, similar age, similar values, same motivations," she says. This is the power of collaboration. When we bring our distinct gifts to the table, we all rise.

Contrast this with a small town I visited where nearly every shop sold ice cream. One business found success, and others followed, creating an oversaturated market. Imagine if they'd each leaned into offering a unique corner of the market—baked goods, a charm bar, fresh flowers. Instead of copying success, they could've complemented each other and created a destination where everyone thrives. That's the power of community over competition.

As Heather Slack of *The Post & Office* puts it, "We've never looked at the other businesses in town as competition. It's always been complementary to each other. The more people we can bring to town the better for us. We're all here to work together and we're all here to support each other, we're not here to compete with each other." Collaboration done right fuels growth, not division.

Josh and Laura Scheutzow of *The Kilbourne Project* embody this spirit of collaboration, investing their life savings to transform a historic Ohio town. Together with three other couples, they're building a destination that invites other similar businesses to join the revival. "We're not big developers," Josh says. "We want other like-minded businesses to come to town and be a part of this."

Here's the thing: Success isn't about staring at someone else's highlight reel and trying to copy it. It's not about following the crowd or letting their wins dictate your next move. When you spend time focusing on the competition, you lose sight of yourself and what you're called to do. It pulls you away from your purpose, and your business pays for it. The secret is figuring out what *your* version of success looks like—your wild, messy, one-of-a-kind vision—and chasing it with everything you've got. "How important is it to work together and to create and cultivate ideas together without worrying that anyone's feelings are going to be hurt or that you're stepping on toes," says Kayla White of *Promise Manor* in Lynchburg, Tennessee.

When a small business community unites around a vision, amazing things happen. My friends Melissa Nelson and Marissa Molland dreamed up *Rural Route Ramble*, a small-town "shop hop" across rural Siouxland to highlight and promote small, rural business owners. The event brings thousands of shoppers into small towns across Northwest Iowa during the height of the holiday season, and it grows every year. *Rural Route Ramble* exemplifies the true power of collaboration and working together. "We live out here in the rural part of the state, we love our small towns, and we wanted people that maybe live in a more populated area to see what we have going on out here," says Melissa. "We look at all our vendors and people in tiny towns having businesses that are so cool, and we just want to show people that." These efforts show collaboration's power to spark thriving communities.

In Colby, Kansas—a popular tourist stop along the I-70 corridor—I witnessed a community unite through a *Rural Revival* visioning workshop. Over two days, we brought together four local groups that had separate and sometimes competing goals. After pushing through some challenges, attendees came to understand the assignment and collaborated to create a common vision and define their ideal customer. It was incredibly powerful to see everyone come together and align around a common goal, proving that when one group thrives, the whole town wins.

Community over competition is a movement—showing up, celebrating wins, and building something bigger together.

Because when we all work together, it can be an unstoppable force.

SCARCITY MINDSET VS. ABUNDANCE MINDSET

In small towns, limited resources, few buildings, and small populations can cast a shadow of scarcity, making it feel as if there are never enough customers, opportunities, or success to go around. This "small" thinking can seep into everything: your business, relationships, dreams, and even your sense of possibility. If you're not careful, scarcity becomes a lens that taints your vision, chaining you to fear and competition.

But what if every business could thrive in your town? What if collaboration, not rivalry, was the key to unlocking endless potential? The difference lies in choosing between a scarcity mindset and an abundance mindset—a choice that reshapes how you live, work, and dream.

In case you're not familiar with these terms, I'll explain. A scarcity mindset hoards resources, fears competition, and plays small. But an abundance mindset shares freely, welcomes rivals as allies, and dreams big. Let's see how each of these mindsets view life.

★

SCARCITY MINDSET

- There's never enough to go around, and I fear there never will be.
- I must compete to stay ahead, seeing others as rivals for limited resources.
- I hoard resources and guard my knowledge, suspicious of others' intentions.
- I resent competition, fearing it'll replace me, and blame external factors for my struggles.
- I focus on what's going wrong, believing things will continue to fail.
- I play small, avoid risks, and settle for less, trapped in fixed thinking.
- My piece of the pie is shrinking, and I'm focused on surviving today.

★

ABUNDANCE MINDSET

- There's always more than enough to go around, and I believe in endless possibilities.
- I collaborate to thrive, working with others toward shared goals.
- I share knowledge and resources freely, trusting and uplifting others.
- I embrace competition—it sharpens my edge and drives personal growth.
- I focus on solutions and what's working, filled with optimism and hope.
- I dream big, take bold risks, and commit to learning and development.
- My piece of the pie is growing, and I'm grateful for the opportunities ahead.

This is about more than just mindsets—it's a revolution in how we build in rural America. An abundance mindset overcomes scarcity's limits with a fresh perspective, uncovering opportunities and turning small towns into thriving hubs of connection. Take Sara Ostrander, of *The Centennial* tearoom in Jefferson, Iowa. "We really try to support and prop up other businesses because they've done such a good job supporting us," she says. "It's a good partnership for everybody." By cross-promoting with local shops, Sara's business didn't just survive a massive flood and rebuild—it became a cornerstone of a stronger, more vibrant town.

Dan Douglas of *Belleville Hometown Lumber* echoes this mindset. "We all need to be supportive of local businesses," he says. "Whether it's our business, the grocery store, or restaurants, we depend on local revenue. Any way I can help—encouraging someone or cross-promoting—I'm in." His commitment to lifting others, from mentoring new entrepreneurs to promoting neighboring stores, shows how an abundance mindset creates a ripple effect, sustaining jobs and community pride.

This same spirit shines in Cody, Wyoming, where Jesse Renfors of *Cody Coffee* encouraged collaboration with other coffee shops. "Getting involved in your community is everything," he says. "I try to work with all the coffee shops in town. If we help each other out and keep dollars local, all boats rise." His approach—sharing customers and ideas—has turned competition into camaraderie, creating a culture in Cody that serves locals and visitors alike.

When you're stuck in a scarcity mindset, it makes someone else's win feel like your loss. It breeds isolation, envy, and small thinking, draining the joy from your work. On the flip side, an abundance mindset is a rising tide that lifts everyone. This mindset chooses to see every new and existing business as a partner, not a threat. It's Dan Douglas's passion for cross-promotion, saying, "Anything we can do to encourage or support growth, whether with a young person or another business, we're all about it." It's sowing generosity—sharing tips, collaborating on events, or celebrating a neighbor's success—and watching it grow a thriving community.

What can an abundance mindset look like for you? Start small but think big. Partner with a local shop for a pop-up event. Mentor an aspiring entrepreneur. Share a competitor's win on social media. These acts build trust, loyalty, and growth. Because there's room not only for those already in the game, there's also room for those who want to join it.

Take a long, hard look at how you live and the mindset that drives your actions. Then consider how your mindset affects your view of community over competition. Are you clutching opportunities tightly, fearing a shrinking piece of the pie? Or are you sowing generosity, trusting there's enough for all? Scarcity builds walls; abundance builds bridges.

Choose an abundance mindset and watch how it transforms your life and community. In a world that often feels small, an abundance mindset makes the possibilities endless.

FIND YOUR TRIBE

The people you surround yourself with will help shape your destiny, like threads carefully woven into the fabric of your life. Dreams planted in the right environment will thrive, while those planted in the wrong environment will wither. That's why curating a circle of "dream believers"—positive, inspiring people who champion your success—is critical. These are your "business besties" and mentors—the ones who get the entrepreneurial grind, challenge your ideas, and propel you toward your potential. It's not about using people or "working your connections" but about partnering together to live out your callings in ways you might not achieve alone. Instead of asking, "What can you do for me?" shift your perspective to, "How can we lift each other up?"

The wild ride of entrepreneurship is infinitely better with a solid tribe of people who "get you" by your side. While you can go it alone, having the right people to cheer you on is key to unlocking your potential. Your "business besties"—those who share your vision, celebrate your wins, and call you out when needed—are the secret sauce to leveling up. They're not just a support network; they're catalysts for growth, offering the emotional support and strategic backing that help you thrive.

As entrepreneur Katie Adams of *Stuart Flowers & Gifts* says, "Success is having a collaborative group here in town. You start talking, become friends, and turn into trusted advisors because you trust each other. That's success—because then we're building this community together." A crew like that turns dreams into reality.

Through *Rural Revival*, I've seen many versions of this concept come to life. Strangers turn into real-life friends, connecting over shared visions or business ideas, cheering each other on, and making each other better. There's nothing more rewarding than watching these bonds form.

Your business besties are the ones who see you, share your fire, and push you to think bigger. As Anne Greenwalt notes, "Entrepreneurship is really hard. You can feel alienated because your friends don't quite get what you're going through if they don't own a business." Finding fellow entrepreneurs who understand the late nights and the thrill of a win is a game-changer. They make you feel seen and keep you motivated.

Those quick, three-minute calls—where you hash out a problem and move on—are like walking into a colleague's office in a traditional workplace. Iron sharpens iron, and surrounding yourself with people who understand the hustle makes all the difference.

Mentors, meanwhile, are like a fast pass on your entrepreneurial journey. A single conversation with the right mentor can save you years of trial and error. Libby Timmerman of *Heart & Sole Dance and Performing Arts Studio* puts it perfectly: "Living in a small town, go find any business owner and say, 'Can I sit down and talk with you? How did you do this?' They'll help—I guarantee it. Because they all started in the exact same place." A thirty-minute chat with a mentor can be worth more than a library of business books. They provide direction, resources, and doors to new possibilities. They help protect you from mistakes, provide invaluable wisdom, and are oftentimes willing to promote you and send opportunities your way. Mentors empower you to walk out your purpose effectively, filling in gaps you didn't even know you had.

But not everyone belongs in your circle. Take a hard look at your relationships. Are you surrounded by people who dream big? Or those who settle for less and always complain that "nothing good ever comes my way"? Dream squashers—those negative voices who project their own fears, doubts, and insecurities onto you or tear each other down—can drain your energy and derail your vision. In contrast, dream believers inspire you to dream bigger as they offer positivity and possibility. When you surround yourself with fellow dreamers, you start to dream again.

As the saying goes, you become most like the people you spend the most time with. If you want to upgrade your future, start by upgrading your circle. Instead of getting stuck in the town gossip group text, seek out people who talk about big ideas, growth, and dreams. This gossip—all too common in small towns—is draining. But vision expands and opens minds to bigger and better possibilities. If you want to break through, you may need to break away from those limiting voices.

Sometimes, finding your tribe requires you to step outside your bubble—join a Mastermind group, connect with entrepreneurs online, or get more involved in your local community. Our *Rural Revival* community is a great place to start. Be intentional about connecting with people who share your values, and don't be afraid to give as much as you get. Share ideas, celebrate wins, and stay connected with a quick coffee or check-in.

If you don't yet have these people in your life and don't know where to find them, start by praying. Ask God for divine appointments that will connect you with those meant to be part of your tribe—people who will partner with you to fulfill your call. And then watch as He starts to bring them into your life— because I promise, He will.

Entrepreneurship can feel lonely, but it doesn't have to. Your business besties and mentors are more than a support system— they're the key to building a legacy. They challenge you, help solve problems, and inspire you to keep pushing. The older I get, the more I treasure relationships that sharpen me. So, go find your tribe—those who see life bigger than themselves, who lift others up, and who are ready to help you conquer the world. Lean into the power of community and watch how far you can go together.

GO BEYOND THE LOCALS: EXPAND YOUR DIGITAL FOOTPRINT

Social media provides an incredible opportunity to connect with your local audience and build an amazing community far beyond your zip code—especially in small towns where opportunities can feel limited. But social media can be a double-edged sword. Approach it with the right mindset, and it can transform your relationships and livelihood. Let it consume you, and it becomes a trap. We've all been there—heads down, endlessly scrolling, chasing likes, followers, or the next viral moment. Meanwhile, real-life connections, the ones right in front of us, take a backseat. The good news is that you don't *have* to choose between social media and real-life connections. My challenge to you is to make the most of *both* opportunities. The way to do this is to adjust your mindset.

When you focus on connection, social media isn't just a platform—it's a bridge to people who inspire, support, and share your vision. Don't limit yourself by chasing metrics. No matter how many followers or likes you have, you'll never feel that you have enough. Instead, shift your focus to the community you *do* have. Engage with them. Show up authentically. Like Jasmin Stidham's strategy—prioritize relationships over numbers to build lasting connections that fuel success.

Here's how to keep a winning mindset in your approach to social media:

- **Be faithful in the small things.** Respond to comments, answer messages, and show gratitude for the people who show up for you. These small actions create ripple effects.

- **Build community, not just a following.** Social media isn't a substitute for real-life connection but a tool to enhance it. Use it to spark conversations, share your story, and uplift others.

- **Let go of comparison.** Your worth isn't tied to your follower count. Celebrate your community, no matter the size, and watch it grow organically.

- **Set boundaries to keep it healthy.** Social media should serve you, not own you. Engage intentionally, then step away to invest in the people around you.

Social media is what you make of it. Use it to connect, inspire, and grow—without letting it define you. Focus on people—building relationships and community. Show up for them, stay grounded, and watch your business grow. Profits will follow.

DREAM ON, TOGETHER

When you sit at the table with the dreamers, the movers and shakers, the warriors, the ones who fight for others, the conversation takes on a whole new meaning. It breathes life into you as a business owner in ways nothing else can.

As we learn and grow, the conversations we crave begin to change. We've done the surface talk. We've sat at the tables that looked great but didn't feel right. But now we seek something deeper. We want to be around those who dream out loud. Who dare to hope, build, and rebuild. Who've known pain yet kept their fire. Who talk about purpose, growth, joy, and legacy. Who build with integrity. Because when we sit at those tables—with the ones who've lived, lost, learned, and loved fiercely—we don't just feel seen. We remember what really matters. And suddenly, we're not just passing time, not just surviving—we're learning how to thrive. What a way to live!

As small business owners, one of the greatest things we can do is support each other—buy from local shops, shout out fellow entrepreneurs on social media, collaborate on events. As Lynne Thomas of *Barnstorm Coffee* says, "People are so generous with their time, and they really want to help you succeed." When we sow into our communities, the rewards will multiply.

As the saying goes, "If you want to go fast, go alone. If you want to go far, go together." So, start building your dream and take some people along for the ride.

Invest in passionate people with vision. Protect your dream by avoiding dream squashers and seek out dream believers who fuel your fire. Who you surround yourself with shapes your destiny, so find your business besties and mentors and make them part of your business plan.

Your tribe is out there, waiting to help you carve your path. Go find them and watch how far you can go—together!

★

ACTIVATION

Who are the people who champion your dreams and push you to grow?

How can you create a community of dream believers this week?

What's one way you can collaborate with a local business to strengthen your town?

Where do you notice a scarcity mindset in your business or life? How can you replace it with an abundance mindset?

CHAPTER EIGHT

IT'S NOT THE CRITIC
WHO COUNTS

★

*"It is not the critic who counts; not the man who
points out how the strong man stumbles, or
where the doer of deeds could have done them
better. The credit belongs to the man who strives,
who dares greatly, and who perseveres; who
spends himself in a worthy cause; who at the best
knows in the end the triumph of high
achievement, and who at the worst, if he fails, at
least fails while daring greatly, so that his place
shall never be with those cold and timid souls
who neither know victory nor defeat."*
— *The Man in the Arena, by Theodore Roosevelt*

I wish I could promise that chasing your small-town dream
will unfold like a heartwarming movie—your community
waving pom-poms, cheering your every step, and bringing your
vision to life, set to a soundtrack of inspiring moments. But if
I'm being genuinely honest, big dreams often meet resistance,

especially in places that maybe haven't had a big dream for a while.

I hear this story over and again from the small-town entrepreneurs who have staked their claims on Main Street USA. They understand that resistance doesn't arise because their dreams lack value. Rather, it's a result of the discomfort their dreams create in those who find comfort in the familiar.

When you pour your heart, time, and energy into a bold vision, you too might struggle with doubters or skeptics who are hesitant to embrace something new.

This chapter is here to provide a safe space for that struggle. It's not about denying or ignoring the challenge but wrapping you in encouragement and support to keep you moving forward. Resistance doesn't define your worth—it's a sign you're in the arena, daring greatly. It means you're stirring the promise of what's possible. So, keep going. Your dream is worth fighting for, and your town needs your hope.

THE SMALL-TOWN ECOSYSTEM

Every small town has an unspoken ecosystem—a network of roles that keeps things running smoothly in a familiar way. Over time, this system takes shape, with many pouring their hearts and effort into their communities, creating something truly meaningful. Often, we don't notice this ecosystem until a new idea stirs. But when someone steps up with a new vision, it can send ripples through this ecosystem, touching those who've settled into the comfort of how things are.

As a dreamer full of vision, you might encounter gatekeepers who value their influence, volunteers who cherish recognition, or others who thrive in the spotlight. Your passion, like a light in a quiet room, might challenge their sense of place or highlight their reluctance to embrace change. Their resistance isn't always about you—it's often about their own discomfort with change or fear of losing their role.

When you pursue the vision in your heart, it might shift the familiar rhythm. Some may feel unsettled, not because your idea isn't good, but because it prompts them to reflect on their own potential. They might think, *I could've done more*, and that reflection can feel uncomfortable. Instead of rising to meet the challenge, a few might try to hold you back, not out of malice, but to stay in their comfort zone or established role.

Sometimes, people don't see the purpose for your life because they're still searching for their own purpose. They might worry your dream overshadows theirs, a hint of that scarcity mindset sneaking in. Others may believe, *This is as good as it gets*, hesitant to hope for more. Some might want their names tied to your vision because they're wrestling with their own need for recognition. These reactions actually aren't even about you or your dream, they reflect that person's own journey.

This reality can feel surprising, even disheartening. You're out there trying to uplift your community, so why isn't everyone rallying beside you? Why does your passion meet hesitation instead of excitement? If you're reading this book, you've likely felt the resistance too. You're pushing against the invisible ecosystem that's settled over your town, and it stirs up some feelings—even when your idea is purely for the community's good. Change can feel personal, or even like a challenge to those comfortable with the way things are. The situation can be frustrating, even heartbreaking, because their resistance doesn't just hurt you—it holds back the entire community.

THE ROOTS OF RESISTANCE

Because we care so much about our small towns, it's easy to find many emotions woven into the fabric of any close-knit community. There's love, community pride, and loyalty that bind us tight. Other emotions can spark resistance when new ideas challenge familiar ways because they are rooted in comparison, jealousy, ego, intimidation, and fear. These emotions aren't unique to rural America; they're universal human struggles that surface when change disrupts the familiar. Let's further explore these roots to help understand why pushback happens, and how to rise above it to move our communities forward.

Comparison can cloud connection. Someone who could be your ally might feel a tug of rivalry, thinking, *I wish that idea was mine*. It's not always intentional—it's often a struggle with their own sense of worth. If they knew how valued they are, they could cheer for you. As the saying goes, "When you're secure in who you are, you can celebrate who others are." Keep shining, let others know you value what they bring to the table, and you'll make space for everyone's gifts to grow.

Jealousy is a quiet struggle that often slows a town's progress. When someone sees your dream or passion, they might think, *Why them and not me?* A scarcity mindset whispers, *There's not enough success to share*. But that's not true! Opportunities are limitless if we'll just seek them out. As the Bible says, God is no respecter of persons—if He's working through you, He can work through them too. Their jealousy doesn't only hurt you—it holds back the good your town could share. Respond with kindness and compassion, extend grace and forgiveness to those who struggle in this area, and stay focused on your path to keep your town moving forward.

Ego often hides behind pride. When you share a bold idea, some might feel their place in the town is challenged, thinking,

I've been here longer—why should you lead the charge? It's not about your dream's value but their need to feel significant or be the loudest voice in the room. They may try to steer your efforts, downplay your ideas, or seek control to protect their sense of importance. But true significance comes from God and living out His purpose for your life, not from outshining others. If ego creates resistance, stay humble, keep your heart on your call, and let your actions speak and show the way forward.

Intimidation can feel heavy. Your courage might make others feel their hesitation is exposed, as if your vision highlights a step they haven't taken. *Who are you to change things?* they might wonder. Again, not because your idea is wrong, but because it stirs their insecurities. Whether you're launching a business, reviving a community space, or trying new things, your initiative can feel like a mirror to their doubts—and that reflection feels uncomfortable. They're not just questioning your plan; they're wrestling with their own fears of falling short. Keep the faith, trust your vision, and see their intimidation as a sign your vision is stirring something powerful.

Fear of change can seem daunting, especially in towns where tradition feels comfortable and familiar. Holding onto what "used to be" feels safe, but giving new life to old spaces means stepping into the unknown, which can feel scary and overwhelming. That fear might show up as a comment at a town meeting, distance from a former ally, or reluctance to embrace your plans. It's not always personal—just a human instinct to stay comfortable. But their fear doesn't define your calling. God placed that dream in your heart for a reason, and no amount of resistance can take away its purpose. Keep moving, trusting your courage can inspire others to face their fears and join the journey toward a brighter future.

These roots reflect the natural push and pull of change in a town's ecosystem and often stem from a lack of hope. Understanding these roots can help you navigate pushback with kindness. Your role is to stay focused on your purpose and let others' doubts fade into the distance. Don't let their hesitation dim your light. As Kim Ellenz of *Old School Seals* reminds us, "For every voice of doubt, there are more cheering you on." Keep moving forward with kindness, showing your town what's possible when you dare to dream. Your vision doesn't take away from anyone—it opens the door for everyone to rise and invites everyone to dream bigger.

THE NAYSAYERS' NOISE

The world is full of critics eager to tell you why your dream won't work. But here's the truth: I've seen the wildest dreams absolutely thrive in rural America. The craziest ideas—ones that might seem destined to fail by some—can thrive when passion meets purpose. You don't need directions from people who've never been where you're going, because they don't have your map. It's time to blaze your own trail.

I've had my fair share of raised eyebrows when I share what I do. "That's your *job*?" they ask, like I'm chasing some sort of pipe dream or fantasy. But I've learned to lean into the passions that keep me up at night, the ones God planted in my heart that make me feel alive—because those are the dreams worth fighting for. I've learned to quiet the voices that don't understand or make me wonder, *What will people think?*

Perhaps you too have faced such skeptics. They often don't see the power of risk and reward. Where they see a mountain and turn back, you see the mountain and start climbing. Every path has resistance—but that's part of the journey. Do what you love, pour your heart into it, and build a life around it. Because the people counting you out? They aren't *your* people. When your work aligns with your purpose, it doesn't just feel like work—it feels worth it, no matter what others might say.

There comes a moment where you must decide: You can give in to the loud voices telling you it can't work or why someone else should take the lead—or you can stop letting others hold the key to your own joy. When you choose the latter, everything changes. You'll stop chasing approval, stop listening to the voices that steal your peace, and stop worrying about who is with you, against you, or too afraid to pick a side. Instead, you will move forward, trusting your heart and chasing the dream that sets you alive. This is your new standard—living boldly, unapologetically, for the calling that sets your soul on fire.

When the naysayers' noise gets loud, let Asher Roth's words be louder: "Do your thing. Do it unapologetically. Don't be discouraged by criticism. You probably already know what they're going to say. Pay no mind to the fear of failure. It's far more valuable than success. Take ownership, take chances, and have fun. And no matter what, don't ever stop doing your thing."

Don't let critics—even those closest to you—hold back your calling. They might prefer the old you—perhaps the high school version of you or the version that buried dreams instead of chasing them—but God is calling you to version 2.0. Instead of focusing on what others say about you, focus on what God says about you and growing into who you're meant to be.

Ask yourself these questions: *What does God say about me? How does God feel about my dream? What is His plan for me? How can I get past what other people have put on me?*

You're not here to win everyone's approval, you're here to live your calling. Let others' doubts fuel your fire. Keep building, keep daring, and let the results speak.

WHEN THINGS DON'T GO AS PLANNED

Sometimes, despite all your efforts or how great your dream is, a town just isn't ready for your vision. Maybe the people are deeply rooted in the past, hesitant to imagine a new, brighter future. Maybe local leaders resist change, or some—as hard as it is to believe—would rather see the town fade than see a dream flourish. That resistance can feel heavy, but it doesn't mean your dream is dead.

Stay open to new possibilities. Think outside the box. Consider nearby towns that might welcome your idea with open arms. Try a different approach, a new location, or connect with a fresh circle of collaborators. Flexibility doesn't mean giving up —it means trusting God's plan might take a different route, even if it's not the path you first imagined.

This detour doesn't mean you'll never bring your dream home to the town you love. It just means the timing or the setting might not be right yet. Don't let that detour slow you down. Chase a version of your vision—maybe in a neighboring town, a different building, or with new partners. Be open to a route you didn't expect. Because that unexpected path? It might open a door to something even greater.

Trust that good things can come from a different path, too. Your courage to keep moving forward, even when plans shift, can light the way for your dream to thrive and inspire others along the way.

BE AN AGENT OF HOPE

In small towns, you'll almost always find the whisper of "that's not how we do things here," the skepticism that greets big dreams, or the comfort of settling for "what's always been" somewhere in the vicinity. This small-town mindset can bring a feeling of hopelessness, holding people back from imagining a brighter future. But you? You're called to move beyond those limits. You're sent to be an agent of hope, a living reminder that transformation is possible, no matter the odds.

Being an agent of hope means igniting possibility in others through your actions, words, and unwavering belief in what could be. It's about seeing beyond the obstacles and inspiring those around you to do the same. When you embrace this role, it changes not only how you see your community, but how others see it. Let these ideals be your roadmap:

- **Live boldly with purpose.** Let your values and passions guide you. When you chase your dreams—whether launching a small business, learning a new craft, or championing a local cause—you show others what's possible, even in a small town where skeptics may doubt you. Your courage becomes a beacon, proving that purpose can triumph over fear.

- **Weave a stronger community.** Create spaces where people feel seen and valued. Consider hosting a coffee meetup, boosting a local entrepreneur on social media, or organizing a community event. Inspired by the small-town camaraderie you admire, foster collaboration over competition. A simple act such as rallying neighbors to brainstorm solutions shows how everyone's light can shine brighter together.

- **Listen deeply, lift higher.** When someone shares their struggles or dreams, listen with your heart and affirm their potential. Be the encourager who pours "gasoline on dreams" with kind words or practical guidance, helping others see possibilities they've overlooked.

- **Embrace resilience with optimism.** Setbacks are real, but so is your ability to rise above them. When skeptics question your path, stay anchored in your purpose. Share how you've pushed through challenges to remind others that hope endures, turning obstacles into steppingstones.

- **Spread hope through generosity.** Small acts—such as shopping local, volunteering at a county fair, or mentoring someone—create ripples of change. Your generosity shows that giving without expecting anything in return can lift an entire community, one kind gesture at a time.

- **Inspire a brighter future.** Share a hopeful vision for your town, whether in a conversation at the local diner, in a local meeting, or through the example you set. Emphasize possibility over limits, helping others see a future where your community thrives.

- **Anchor hope in faith.** When faith is your foundation, it will fuel your hope. Draw strength from what grounds you, inspiring others to keep believing even when some doubt.

As an agent of hope, you don't just see what could be—you help others see it too. You're not held back by what stands in the way, you're driven by purpose and empowered by what's possible. As Sandy Schubert of *Hedgie's Books* says, "Make a commitment that you're gonna love your town even on the hard days. You have to find a way to help it succeed."

You're called to be an agent of hope, anchored in God's purpose, showing your town what's possible when you dare greatly. Start small and watch how these sparks of hope can transform your community, lighting the way for others to follow.

CREATE A YES CULTURE

In small towns, it's easy for a "no" mindset to take hold. You've heard it before: "That's not how things work here," or "Why bother trying?" Such comments are not always rooted in cynicism—they just may be the result of people worn down by years of setbacks or afraid to dream bigger. That kind of thinking can hold you back, dimming the spark of what's possible. But here's the good news: You can change that "no" mindset. You have the chance to build a culture that says "yes" to new ideas and bold visions, starting with the people you surround yourself with and the way you show up in your community.

I discovered a very inspiring *yes culture* in Courtland, Kansas, a town of 291 people with a thriving Main Street. As Luke Mahin of *Irrigation Ales* shared, "They've always been a progressive community. We've never been told this is not gonna work. Instead, we got asked for three years, when are you opening?" That mindset dropped Courtland's median age from fifty-five to the thirties and sparked the first population increase in fifty years. This kind of mindset is exactly what we need more of in our small towns. Luke adds, "If we're joining all these other people putting blood, sweat, and tears into the town, there's tons of reasons to build into this ecosystem."

Here's how you can create a *yes culture* in your town, turning doubt into hope one step at a time:

- **Find your yes people.** Surround yourself with those who lift you up and share your vision—dreamers and doers who say, "Let's make it happen," instead of "That'll never work." These yes people are the mentors, neighbors, or friends with big ideas who fuel your drive, not those who raise doubts. Find them, lean on them, and build your team of encouragers.

- **Challenge the no mentality.** When someone says, "That won't work here," don't buy it. Take inspiration from Andrea Stordahl, who was told, "Businesses don't survive in this town." She proved them wrong, building a vibrant community hub despite the skeptics. You can do the same —share your idea at the local diner, pitch a project at a town meeting, or give a shoutout to a local entrepreneur. Each step chips away at the old way of thinking and shifts the conversation toward possibility.

- **Lead with *yes* or *maybe*.** Take inspiration from places like Courtland, Kansas, a town that chooses to say *yes* or *maybe* before it says *no*. Be that voice in your town, asking "Why not?" or cheering on someone's big idea. Create a culture that says *yes* to possibility—because it's contagious.

- **Build momentum, step by step.** Changing a town's mindset is a long game, especially when doubt has been around for decades. But every action counts, and when momentum grows, it can become unstoppable. Host a community potluck, promote a local shop online, or mentor someone with a dream. These small acts of belief plant seeds for a future where possibility thrives.

Building a *yes culture* is about saying, "Let's try it!" instead of "That's not for us." It's about creating a town where hope wins over doubt and people lift each other up. So, start today— find one *yes* person, support one idea, take one small step. It might not happen overnight because oftentimes you're trying to change mindsets that have been in place for decades. But keep your eye on the prize and start making changes now that can reap massive rewards in the future. Over time, your efforts will rewire the heart of your town, turning it into a place where dreams don't just survive—they soar.

DON'T WAIT FOR THE APPLAUSE

Ever notice how one harsh comment can drown out a dozen kind words? In a small town, those negative voices can feel overwhelming, making it hard to believe anyone's rooting for you. It's tempting to stay stuck, waiting for the crowd to cheer before you take a step. But here's the truth: You don't need their applause to chase the dream in your heart.

It can be lonely stepping out to chase a dream before the crowd catches up. And that's the catch: Most people cheer only when your success appears certain, when it's safe to believe in you. Those naysayers aren't always trying to tear you down. Sometimes they're just stuck in the comfort of the familiar, wary of anything new. Their doubts can make you question your own passion, and I'm sorry if their words have dimmed your light or pulled you off your path. But those limits they try to set? They can't hold you.

Waiting for everyone's approval only keeps your dreams on hold. Instead, tune out the noise and trust what you know is possible. Like so many stories shared on the *Rural Revival* podcast—people who have built thriving community hubs despite being told their town was dying—you can prove the skeptics wrong by moving forward.

Your true supporters are out there, and more are coming— people who will lift you up, quietly cheering and ready to help. So don't wait for everyone to get on board. Start right now, right where you are. Just like the *yes culture* you're helping to build, this is about focusing on what's possible, not what's in the way. Every step you take plants a seed of hope, showing your community that dreams can take root here. The negative voices will fade as you keep going, and your people will find you.

THE ONES WHO LIFT YOU UP

Some days, it feels as if the world is shouting at you to play it safe, to shrink your dreams to fit someone else's comfort zone. Whether from a neighbor's sideways glance or a critic's harsh words—those voices can make you second-guess your path. But you weren't made to stay small. The key is finding the people who see your vision and lift it higher, those who remind you that your dreams are worth chasing. These are the people who fuel your courage and say, "Keep going, you've got this," no matter how hard it gets.

Surround yourself with those who lift you up, not drag you down. Steer clear of the drama or competitive vibes that try to hold you back. Some people might push back because your vision reminds them of dreams they haven't chased. But if their lives don't reflect the dream you're building, their doubts don't get to steer you. Your true supporters—those who want what's best for you and believe in your potential—are out there, and God is sending them one by one. He might send a neighbor, a new face, a friend or a mentor, to root for you and talk you up behind your back. Even when it feels like you're on your own, your supporters are there, cheering in the background.

Your dream is yours for a reason, so chase it with everything you've got. Let the critics talk. Because no matter what they throw at you, they'll never have your purpose and your passion. Fight to keep it, because you're the only one who can bring your dream to the world. Be so busy building, daring greatly, and being an agent of hope that those negative voices fade into the background while you focus on what's ahead. The credit belongs to you—the one in the arena, face marred by dust and sweat, striving for a worthy cause. Keep loving your town, even on the tough days. Your purpose is bigger than others' doubts, and it will make a difference if you keep going.

★

ACTIVATION

Who are the people in your community who share your vision? How can you connect with them to build a stronger support circle?

Where have you bumped into your small town's ecosystem, and how can you overcome obstacles it may be creating?

Think of a time when you faced resistance to a new idea. How can you reframe that pushback as a chance to grow and inspire others?

How can you start creating a yes culture in your community?

What's one way you can show up as an agent of hope in your town?

What personal value or strength keeps you anchored when critics question your path, and how can you draw on it to keep moving forward?

CHAPTER NINE

FROM SURVIVING TO THRIVING

★

*"Twenty years from now you will be more
disappointed by the things that you didn't do than
by the ones you did do. So throw off the bowlines,
sail away from safe harbor, catch the trade winds in
your sails. Explore, Dream, Discover."*

— *Mark Twain*

If you're running a small business in a rural town, you've already done something brave—you chased a dream and opened your doors. But let's be real. Sometimes it feels like you're just keeping your head above water, barely breaking even, hoping to make it through another month. You're not alone. I've met so many small-town entrepreneurs who feel the same.

Too many small-town business owners equate survival with success. They've chased their dreams, opened their doors, and now they're just getting by—covering costs but not making a profit, winging it, settling for "good enough."

That scarcity mindset whispers, *This is as good as it gets.* It traps you in predictability, getting by on just enough instead of reaching for more. For many rural business owners, this mindset manifests as settling for breaking even because "it's helping the community" or "it's my dream, even if it doesn't pay." But surviving isn't thriving, and God calls us to step into abundance, not limitation.

To thrive, you must let go of the belief that you can't make money and follow your passion at the same time—because you *can* do both! You can love your community, serve with your whole heart, and run a profitable business. I don't want you to just keep the lights on. I want you to build a business that lights up your life and your community—personally and professionally. The ten strategies below will help you clarify your focus, refine your approach, and build a business that doesn't just survive but soars. Because surviving isn't the goal. Thriving is.

1. Link Your Passion and Purpose with Profit. Building a thriving business means weaving together passion, purpose, and profit. Passion—what sets your soul on fire—drives you to keep going. Purpose, your *why*, roots your work in meaning, such as serving your neighbors or breathing life into your Main Street. Profit isn't the goal alone; it's the engine that sustains your vision, creating jobs and opportunities that lift your town. Purpose and passion alone will not build a sustainable business —but linking purpose and passion with profit will.

Start to look at ways you can monetize your passion. Ask yourself: *What problem does my business solve?* Whether it's providing fresh goods or creating a community hub, addressing real needs turns passion into impact, builds a profitable business, and strengthens the local economy. This is the sweet spot— weave these three strands together, you create a legacy that's both fulfilling and enduring, proving that in small towns, doing good and doing well go hand in hand.

Keep the balance in check. Review your passion, purpose, and profit alignment quarterly. Make this a priority. Money is always a motivator, but in lean seasons, when profits dip, your passion and purpose will keep you going. For example, my goal with this book is to inspire and empower as many people as possible to chase their dreams. That's what drives me. And when I do that, the profit follows. Yes, there are smart business decisions I can make behind the scenes to ensure I make the most profit possible from every book sold. But the goal is not to sell X number of books so I can make X number of dollars. It's to impact X number of lives so that we can have even more amazing people chasing their dreams in rural America—or so that those who already are can be encouraged and realize how impactful their businesses are. Smart business decisions—such as optimizing book sales or managing inventory—should support this mission but never overshadow it.

Many entrepreneurs, especially creatives, lean heavily on passion but shy away from financial strategy. If this is you, partner with a trusted accountant or financial advisor to bridge the gap. For retail owners, our Dream Builder trainings can help you get profitable in other ways, through strategies such as maximizing store space, effective inventory management, and intentionally building customer relationships for repeat business.

A profitable business looks different for everyone. Define what success means for you—beyond just dollars. Meet with your accountant or banker to align your financial plan with your dream. Profit matters, but it's also often the other things—the community connections, the lives touched—that bring in the dollars and make small town businesses thrive.

ACTION STEP

Grab a pen and paper and set aside some time this week. List out ways to turn your passion into a sustainable business, such as selling a product that meets a local need (e.g., fresh goods, a gathering space) or offering a service that draws visitors. Then write down every way you can possibly think of that could make you money if you connect your purpose and passion to profit. Brainstorm as many ideas as you can. Pull out the best ideas and use them to create a blueprint that outlines your path.

2. Create a Memorable Customer Experience. People everywhere, from small town locals to city visitors, crave a heartwarming experience that feels like stepping into a Hallmark movie. Our small towns offer the perfect setting where your business or project can offer exactly that—whether through a welcoming in-person space or event, or a vibrant online presence.

It's not just about what you offer; it's about how you make people *feel*. Your coffee shop isn't just serving lattes—it's creating a cozy morning ritual. Your boutique isn't just selling dresses—it's helping someone feel confident for a big day. Share your story through a thoughtful shop design, an inviting website, or engaging social media that invites connection. Curate moments that transport people to a meaningful place in their lives.

You don't have to do this alone. Team up with your community—other businesses, schools, or local groups—to make your whole town a destination. Many small towns are just waiting to become that charming, storybook place. All it takes is a little creativity to bring it to life.

Look at Franklin, Tennessee, for example. When I lived in Franklin it was much smaller than it is today. While it may not have fit my criteria for a true small town, it still had that small town vibe—and to some extent, it still does. In many ways it's what every small town aspires to be.

Franklin hasn't always been this way. There was a time when its once thriving Main Street had become quiet, lined with empty storefronts and dated facades. But it still had potential, and the community saw it. Driven by a visionary community group and an increasing population, Franklin's Main Street is once again a bustling hub of shops, restaurants, coffee shops, and a historic theater. Events including the Dickens Christmas festival, Veteran's Day parade, and the Williamson County Fair draw crowds, while dreamy backroads seem like they're straight out of a movie.

My friend Mary Morgan Gentry, a Franklin native who was born and raised on *Gentry's Farm*, shared on my podcast: "I grew up loving Main Street's charm. I always dreamed of owning a shop here, and that dream came true." Franklin's revival shows what's possible when a community leans into its charm and creates experiences that linger in the heart.

Or look at Versailles, Kentucky, nestled in the heart of bourbon and horse country. In 2017, Emily Riddle opened *The Amsden* coffee shop and *Gathered Living* mercantile, breathing life into a town square ripe with potential. Her vibrant displays and curated events—including pop ups, book fairs, and fun experiences for kids—turned downtown Versailles into a destination location. Now, her new project, *The Aldenberg*, a boutique hotel with a restaurant and distillery, adds even more charm and reasons to visit—and stay.

Then there's *Rural Revival*'s farm-to-table dinners that celebrate rural roots. These gatherings, sometimes fundraisers or milestone celebrations, bring communities together and spark momentum. One guest shared, "It's the only time in my life when I felt like I was in the middle of a Hollywood movie. One of my favorite experiences ever!" That's the kind of impact the right experience can make. Or look at *Rural Route Ramble*, where Melissa and Marissa, who we met in chapter 7, put on a fun regional event that's become an annual tradition marked on everyone's calendars. It draws growing crowds excited to shop and celebrate the charm of small-town USA.

These events show how small-town experiences can inspire everyone to build a brighter future. Your creativity can turn your town into a place where people feel connected and inspired, ready to dream bigger together.

ACTION STEP

Brainstorm one way to elevate your customer experience. Could you host a seasonal event, redesign your store's ambiance, or create a social media campaign that tells your brand's story? Partner with local businesses, schools, or organizations to amplify the experience and make your town a destination location.

3. Build a Strong Community. A thriving business is rooted in relationships. When you build a strong community around your brand, you create loyal customers who feel like friends. These connections bring vibrancy to your life and business, while at the same time meeting real needs through your products or services.

Find ways to make your business personal. Learn your customers' names, remember their preferences, or send handwritten thank-you notes. Host events or collaborate with other local businesses for cross-promotions, such as a joint pop-up market or a charity fundraiser. Online, engage authentically through VIP customer groups, social media questions and polls, or newsletters that share your story. As JB Royer of *Royer's Round Top Cafe* in Texas shares, "Relationships take work. And if you really nurture those relationships and the customers that walk through that door, they will time and time again always be there."

Listening is key. Your customers' feedback—what they love, what they need, what excites them—gives you a roadmap for growth. What are they asking for? What's the big new thing they're excited about? When you act on their input, you show them they're heard, which builds loyalty and trust. As Tim Boettner of *A Well Worn Story* explains, "We're always trying to bring something new and fresh. We listen to our customers and what they want, but we also stay true to who we are and our brand."

Michelle Myers, with her fun personality and creative business ideas, has built an amazing community with her *Dirt Road Candle Co.* customers. She's found a way to bring her online business to the farm, offering farm-to-table dinners, special shopping experiences at her shop, and more. Through these events and her engaging (and often hilarious) social media posts, she invites customers into her story. Every post, every event, offers moments of joy and connection. Her efforts show how a business can build a cherished community, lifting everyone up.

Your relationships are the heart of your town's potential. By cultivating authentic connections, you create a space where customers, neighbors, and businesses grow stronger together, making your town a place where everyone thrives.

ACTION STEP

This week, reach out to five customers—ask for feedback, thank them for their support, or invite them to a special event. Build relationships that make your business a bright spot in their day.

4. Embrace Flexibility and Try New Things. Thriving requires adaptability. As your business grows, don't be afraid to experiment, pivot, or diversify. I always say, "I'll try anything once." And I've done that over and over. If an idea works and you're onto something awesome, double down. If it doesn't, you've learned something valuable. Every perceived failure is a lesson that fuels growth.

Revisit your goals every ninety days to stay on track. Are your strategies working? What needs tweaking? Diversify your income streams—could you add a new product, offer a service, or explore an online store? Small adjustments can yield big results.

Take Riley Wymer of *Savannah Sevens* and Brett McPherson of *Designer's Brew*, who met through the *Rural Revival* podcast and teamed up to create a home furnishings line. Their collection stayed true to their brands while expanding their reach in a fresh way. As Brett says, "It's amazing what we can do in life if we just try."

Or think outside of the box like Jaye Wells and *True Ranch Collection*, who transformed the O.T.O. Ranch—a historic Yellowstone dude ranch—into a summer pop-up experience. The lodge and cabins, empty since 1939, were once again filled with authentic western decor and the buzz of guests—all made possible by hauling in everything from decor and china to taxidermy and portable restrooms. It brought back the spirit of the ranch and provided guests an experience they'll never forget.

This visionary approach proves how fresh ideas and creative thinking can bring life and vitality to forgotten spaces.

Rural businesses face unique challenges, but they also offer incredible opportunities to innovate. Taylor Borkowski of *The Cottage* shares, "Being creative with ways to get people in your business right now is our biggest challenge by far. So, we're constantly looking for new, fresh ideas." Steffany Bettin of *BlueJay Boutique* adds, "Adapting to change has been huge. In order to change, you have to stay relevant and give what people want." Rob Grover of *Winghaven Pizza Farm* notes, "There are challenges unique to a rural area, but also incredible opportunities to try something new."

As Matt Dennis and Michael Stepp of *Handlebend*—makers of handcrafted copper mugs—will tell you, "The evolution of our business is, it's just always changing. I think what has surprised us is that we always have something that's pressing and creates its own set of problems that we have to navigate. I guess that's a good thing. I think if you're static, that's probably the beginning of the end, right?" Their experiences demonstrate that flexibility—starting small and adjusting as you learn—keeps your business vibrant, connected, and moving forward.

ACTION STEP

Identify one new idea to try in your business—a pop-up event, a new product line, or a social media campaign. Test it out for thirty days, track the results, and adjust based on what you learn.

5. Look Beyond Your Friends and Family. You've poured your heart into your business, hoping your friends and family would be your biggest cheerleaders. But here's something I've learned: Sometimes, the people closest to you won't understand your vision until it's a proven success—and that's okay. Your biggest fans—the ones who'll rave about your coffee, your candles, or your handmade quilts—might often be strangers who discover the fabulousness you create.

Focus on reaching them—through consistent branding, quality products, and authentic marketing. Build a brand that feels true to you, offer quality that speaks for itself, and share your story authentically. Don't let the silence of familiar faces slow you down—your dream is bigger than that.

Take the guys at *Handlebend* in O'Neill, Nebraska, for example. When they bought a big, historic building for their copper mug business, locals raised their eyebrows. Most knew of *Handlebend*'s mugs but had no idea how much the business was thriving online, reaching customers far beyond O'Neill. As word spread about their bold move, Mike and Matt got what they called "sad eyes" from folks at the grocery store. "Oh, I really hope that works out for you," people would say, and then quietly exit the conversation.

But they didn't let the doubt stop them. They created a space that's more than a bar—it's a community hub where teens hang out and play board games, seniors swap stories, and Saturday nights are filled with chatter and laughter instead of phone screens. Kids run around past bedtime, and the place feels alive. At first, Mike and Matt's biggest supporters weren't their neighbors—they were strangers who fell in love with their products online. Over time, O'Neill caught the vision, and now *Handlebend* draws people from miles away, proving what's possible when you take a risk.

The support you're looking for will come. Keep moving forward and don't let the silence of familiar faces shake your momentum. The people who believe in you are out there, and they will soon be glad they found you.

ACTION STEP

Shift your energy from seeking local validation to reaching your ideal customer. Post about your business on social media, update your website, or run a targeted ad to connect with those who need what you offer.

6. Don't Fear the Sale. Selling is one of those things that is uncomfortable for many, especially in tight-knit rural communities where everyone knows your name, and sometimes "being nice" takes priority over making a profit. I get it. Asking for the sale can feel pushy, like you're bothering people or asking too much. But to thrive as a business, you have to make sales, and sharing what you offer is essential. So, make this simple shift: focus on serving, not selling.

Your business does more than sell—it solves problems, brings joy, or makes life a little brighter. Your bakery isn't just selling bread; it's bringing warmth to a family's table. Your craft shop doesn't just sell supplies; it inspires someone's creativity. Your service isn't merely a transaction; it makes someone's day easier. Your farm stand isn't just about sweet corn, it connects families to fresh, local food. Tell *that* story and selling becomes a way to offer value. By serving your community, you strengthen it.

At *Branded by Rural Revival*, my brand and design business, we don't just build a website and call it a day. We partner with small town entrepreneurs like you to create a brand that is true to your heart. We'll build your website or marketing plan, but we also teach you how to manage it yourself—so you're not stuck paying or waiting on us for every little update. Our business model saves you time and money while giving you freedom to manage your business in a way that works for you. By focusing on serving, not selling, we build trust and lasting relationships, while at the same time setting you up for success.

Embrace selling as a way to help others. As Dakota Dawn Johnson, a seasoned saleswoman and host of the *Cowgirl Confessions* podcast, shares, "If you have a product or service that you know will bless someone else, focus on how it serves them. That gives you the confidence you need." Emily Myers of *Lantana Made* adds, "Be yourself. It's so important to be *you* and to sell that." Your authenticity is your strength—your community wants what you offer, so don't be shy about sharing it.

Your business meets real needs in your town. Don't let it struggle because you are afraid to sell. Remember, you're persuading with a positive purpose. When you focus on how you help others, you'll find confidence to share your value.

ACTION STEP

Practice explaining how your product or service improves lives. Write a short pitch and share it with one customer this week. Frame it as helping, not selling.

7. Don't Treat Your Business Like It's a Charity. Rural America is full of big-hearted people who want to make a difference. It's truly one of our best qualities, if you ask me. You see it in the way we rally for a neighbor in need or put together a bake sale to support a local cause. We care about the people and communities around us, and that's a beautiful part of who we are. But here's a gentle reminder: Giving away too much of your business—your time, products, or services—can stretch your resources too thin, leaving you exhausted and your business at risk. You can be generous while keeping your business strong.

I've seen it too often. A bakery owner who hands out free cookies to every child, thinking it's good for the community. A mechanic fixes everyone's cars for free because that's what a good neighbor does. A florist who gave away so many bouquets for school events that she could hardly pay her rent. She told me, "I just want to be kind." I get it—kindness is at the core of small-town life and acts of kindness are a good thing. But kindness doesn't mean giving your business away. You've worked hard to build this business. It cost you to get where you are. And it's okay to ask customers to value it, too. You can be generous *and* profitable. You can love your community, serve with your whole heart, *and* still send an invoice.

Profitability and purpose go hand in hand. Charging fairly for your time, skills, and creativity ensures you can sustain your vision and keep serving. Your business reflects your hard work and heart—your customers want to support that. Set kind boundaries for your generosity, such as offering a limited number of free items or discounts for special occasions. Determine a dollar amount you're willing to put towards helping your community each year. Don't hold back from sharing the value of what you do. Your business strengthens your town. Keep it sustainable so that you can continue to give for years to come.

ACTION STEP

Set one clear boundary around giveaways, such as "one free sample per customer" or "discounts for loyalty members only." Then, share a short post or tell one customer why your work is worth it.

8. Delegate What Drains You. As a small business owner, you'll likely wear many hats in the early days. But you're not meant to be a one-man or one-woman show forever, especially if you want a business that keeps growing. To scale your business effectively, intentionally delegate tasks you dread or lack expertise in as soon as your finances allow. Hiring for your weaknesses frees up time and energy to focus on what you do best—whether that's creating, strategizing, or leading—and propels your business forward.

Michelle Myers of *Dirt Road Candle Co.* shared, "Hiring someone to handle shipping transformed my business. It gave me the space to dream, create, and focus on what I love." Similarly, Josh Holmquist of *Normal Roasting Company* emphasizes building a strong support network, advising, "Surround yourself with incredible humans... a good leadership team, banker, lawyer, and insurance person... as soon as you're financially able."

Streamline your operations—perhaps use a more cost-effective supplier or use scheduling software to save time. Invest in a professional website as a tool to make your business run smoother. If you need help, our website and design services at *Branded by Rural Revival* can help you build an impactful online presence. Our *Rural Revival* Dream Builder trainings are designed to give you practical tools to build a business that lasts —without sacrificing your heart.

Plan for scalability by envisioning where your business will be in five to seven years and outsourcing tasks that hold you back. By streamlining and delegating strategically, you'll free up time and energy to drive creativity and long-term growth.

ACTION STEP

List the business tasks you love and excel at, and those you dislike or find challenging. Prioritize tasks to delegate as revenue grows, ranking them by time or stress saved, and set financial milestones (e.g., $10,000 monthly revenue to hire a bookkeeper). Research *potential hires, freelancers, or services, noting costs and availability. Track progress and adjust your plan as your business scales.*

9. Keep Your Vision Alive. Building a business in rural America isn't for the faint of heart. There are days when doubt creeps in, when the bank account looks bleak, or when we feel like we're carrying the dream alone. We've all been there, at the end of a hard day, wondering if we made the right call. Late nights, endless to-do lists, and whispers of doubt from others (and ourselves) make it hard. But for me, I keep a note on my desk that says, "Help small town dreamers shine." That's my *why*, my anchor, and it pulls me back every time I waver. Your *why* can do the same for you.

Your vision is what sets your heart on fire. It's why you opened your shop, baked that first loaf of bread, or hung that first sign. But the world is full of voices—well-meaning neighbors, friends, even customers—who'll offer advice that doesn't quite fit. "You should sell this instead," they'll say, or "If you changed this, you'd make more." Their hearts are certainly in the right place, but this is *your* dream, not theirs. Your time, your money, your passion—it's all tied to the vision God planted in you. Stay true to it.

Look at Tia Berens, who runs *The Barn at Aspen Acres*, a wedding and event venue in Spearfish, South Dakota. She told me, "I want to make sure that my vision always aligns with my passion and that I'm producing my passion." Her barn isn't just a venue; it's where couples say, "I do," and start their forever.

Or take Kayla White of *Promise Manor*, who shared, "We don't let a New Years Eve go by without doing a vision board, because creating a vision for your future is when you start to see progress." Tim Boettner of *A Well Worn Story* in New Glarus,

Wisconsin, puts it perfectly. "Stay true to your values and your vision but keep growing and adapting to whatever comes your way. That's the key to lasting."

Your vision is your compass. When slow seasons, negativity, or unsolicited advice come knocking, come back to why you started. Maybe it's to bring joy to your town, provide for your family, or leave a legacy. Whatever it is, hold it close—it's what makes the hard days worth it.

ACTION STEP

Revisit your why *from chapter 4—the heart of why you started your business. Write it down in one sentence. For example, "I want to bring coziness and connection to my town through my coffee shop." Stick it in a place where you'll see it daily—your shop counter, your laptop, or your bathroom mirror. Let it remind you to keep going when things get tough.*

10. Stay Inspired. Inspiration is the spark that keeps your purpose alive, and it often comes from the everyday beauty of the places and community you love. For me, inspiration is found in simple moments—driving down the road with the music turned up or a great podcast sparking new ideas, meeting new people, exploring new small towns, or even discovering creative businesses in bigger cities. These moments recharge my creativity and bring fresh ideas that fuel my work.

You have your own sources of inspiration—perhaps a sunset over open fields, a meaningful conversation, or a favorite hobby —to recharge your creativity. Making time for these moments is essential. Without them, it can be harder to stay energized and creative. By carving out time for what lights you up, you keep your vision clear, and your heart connected to your purpose.

Your inspiration fuels not just your business but your entire town. Whether it's a favorite song, a visit to a new place, or a story that moves you, let these moments recharge you and remind you why you're building something meaningful. Wherever you find your inspiration, make time for it, because it's what keeps your passion alive.

ACTION STEP

This week, take at least one hour to do something that inspires you—whether it's taking a walk in a new place, listening to music that moves you, or visiting a spot that sparks your curiosity. Keep a notebook or phone nearby to jot down any ideas that come to you and reflect on how this moment recharges your creativity.

IF YOU DO WHAT YOU LOVE, THE MONEY WILL FOLLOW

Almost every small-town entrepreneur I've talked to shares this powerful truth: If you do what you love, the money will follow. It won't always happen overnight—trust me, it rarely does. There are lean days, sleepless nights, and moments when you wonder if it's worth it. But if you keep showing up, keep believing, and keep pouring your heart into your work, the rewards will come.

As Grant Golliher of *Diamond Cross Ranch* told me, "You may have to pay a price for a while but hold tight to your vision. Follow your dreams and money will follow you eventually."

Your passion and persistence *will* pay off. You know those desires in your heart aren't random—they're your purpose.

When you step out in faith and take risks, you're not just building a business; you're fulfilling a calling.

Look at James Yates, owner of *Steerfish Steak & Smoke* in Spearfish, South Dakota. His mom gave him some simple advice: "Find what you love and stick with it." That wisdom carried him through slow seasons to build a restaurant that became a community cornerstone, where families laugh and connect over smoky brisket.

Thriving isn't about perfection; it's about progress. You don't need a big city or a big budget to build a thriving business. You need courage, adaptability, and a commitment to serve your community while you value your worth. As Michelle Myers said, "One thing I've learned is that I need to think bigger than what's in front of me." Start small, dream big, and take one step today. Your town—and your future—are waiting for you to make them shine.

Want to host a farm-to-table dinner of your own? Our Farm Dinner Event Kit covers every part of your planning—from organizing volunteers to ticket sales to creating an unforgettable experience for everyone involved, plus tips and tricks we've learned along the way. Get the kit at ruralrevival.co/farmdinner.

Explore our Dream Builder trainings at ruralrevival.co/learn.

★

ACTIVATION

Expand your knowledge. Sign up for one of our Dream Builder trainings at ruralrevival.co/learn to learn practical tools for turning your passion into profit.

Find inspiration. Visit vibrant small towns like Franklin, Tennessee, or Versailles, Kentucky, or grab coffee with a local business owner to spark ideas for a community event.

Share your story. Post one thing about your business online this week—maybe a photo of your product or a quick story about why you love what you do. Your dream customer is out there, waiting to find you.

CHAPTER TEN

WHAT'S THE BEST THAT COULD HAPPEN?

★

"If possible can describe a feeling, that's how I felt. The whole world felt possible. And I was ready for it."
— Elsa Dutton, 1883

Imagine a world where every small town is filled with people living out their purpose—each town buzzing with dreamers building businesses, movements, projects, and communities that reflect their hearts. What a different world it would be. I believe that world is possible—and it starts with dreaming big.

When we chase a dream, we can spend so much time going through worse-case-scenarios and all the ways it could fail. *What's the worst that could happen?* And yes, it's important to be responsible with our planning and a good steward of our resources. But what if we spent as much time focusing on how our dreams could work and the places we could take our dreams if they really did work? What if instead of being consumed by fear, we stepped out in faith and asked ourselves, *What's the best that could happen?*

Take a moment and ask yourself these questions: *If there were no limits, what would I ask God to do in my life? What if I believed He could do it? What if I held on just a little longer for my breakthrough?*

I hope you realize your dream isn't just about you—it's about the impact you make around you. When you live with a vision bigger than yourself, you leave a legacy only God could write.

What's the best that could happen?

ANYTHING IS POSSIBLE

Rural America isn't perfect. As we all know, it has its own unique set of challenges. I'm not here to paint a perfect picture. But I want you to see the possibility. I want you to see opportunity and purpose right where you are.

To those of you who never left, I'm so glad you stayed. This is a new season for you and I'm excited for you to step into it. If you're new to rural America or moving back after some time away, welcome home. I hope you find this is a place where you can live a great life and chase your biggest dreams. I hope your community embraces you with open arms. And I pray you grow to love this place as much as we do.

As I've shared throughout this book, there's been a widespread mentality that we have to settle for less in our small towns. A sense that we must take what's available, because that just might be the best we can do. But in my travels and experiences with *Rural Revival*, I've seen dreamers defy that mindset with stories that will blow you away. When you aim high with a heart for impact, barriers start to crumble. The fulfillment of your dream won't always match your timeline, and things won't always go the way you planned, but with grit and persistence, anything is possible. The stories in this book and on the *Rural Revival* podcast—ordinary people doing extraordinary things—are living proof.

Two of these people are first-generation farmers Josh and Katie Steward of *Steward Farms* in Harrington, Washington. It all started with a letter to an aging farmer and landowner, asking if he might be willing to take a chance and pass on his farm to a young family with a dream to farm. Several years later, the farmer responded, and offered them the chance of a lifetime. In a world where it's nearly impossible to start farming if you don't have a family legacy there, the Stewards defied the odds and saw a dream that seemed impossible come true.

Or consider Eddie and Julie Flores of *Nursing Back to Life* in Lincoln, Kansas. They saw a viral post about a free house in Julie's hometown. They moved the structure and transformed it into a home, repurposing every detail with love. Their project didn't just restore a house—it fueled community pride and inspired others to see possibilities in their town.

These stories show that when you chase the best with the right motives, there's always a way. It might not follow your timeline or your blueprint, but if you keep pushing forward, it *will* happen.

In rural America, we don't just dream the impossible—we *do* the impossible. If you live with the mindset that anything is possible, then anything truly will be possible. You will find a way. It may take some time, it may take a few tries, but you can find your path, I promise. Always aim high, keep believing, and trust that the best is within reach. Because anything is possible— and there are plenty of dreamers out there proving it every day.

What's the best that could happen?

STAY POSITIVE AND FOCUS ON THE WINS

When I moved back home from Nashville and started getting involved in the community, I made a commitment to always speak positively about our town and the projects taking place here. Not just the projects I spearheaded, but the projects others spearheaded too. And through the ups and downs, I've stayed true to that commitment. While it hasn't always been easy, it's been the *right* thing to do. I believe that speaking positive words is one of the keys to bringing hope to the places we live.

Like many of you, I've seen a lot of historic buildings torn down in my town. In my lifetime, there's only been one deteriorating downtown building truly restored and saved. The rest were met with a wrecking ball. When our last remaining two-story building was slated to be next, I saw an opportunity to reverse that trend. With the help of several community members, I started a community foundation to raise funds for our bigger downtown revitalization needs—and that building became our first project.

It was a massive undertaking for a structure that was not in great shape by any means. But through *Rural Revival*, I'd seen worse buildings saved, and I believed anything was possible. So did others. We knew the success of the project could be a turning point for our community, and we spent three years pouring countless hours into the effort. We secured a $100,000 grant and soon a small business stepped up to occupy the space—a perfect opportunity to bring retail back to our town for the first time in decades. Things were looking up.

But dreams don't always go as planned. We were plagued by a crumbling building, multiple storms that further damaged the structure, and a series of roadblocks that prohibited progress. In the end, we couldn't save it. Though we always knew success wasn't guaranteed, the loss stung deeply for everyone who believed in that dream.

Maybe you've found yourself in a similar situation. Maybe you took on a massive project that didn't work out as planned. Maybe you thought you had the support of town leaders, only to face opposition at every turn. Maybe you found more of a scarcity mindset hanging around than you thought. Maybe you bumped into an ecosystem you didn't know existed. Maybe the people you thought would support you instead turned their back or even tried to stop you. Maybe you poured your heart and soul into a dream that didn't work out. Whatever the case, I hope you know it's okay to grieve, but please don't let failure define you.

Easier said than done, right? I get it. Your mind goes through all the what ifs, just as my team and I did. *What if we shouldn't have taken on the biggest project first? What if we'd started smaller? What if we hadn't had to jump through all those hoops and could have moved faster? What if the negative voices had not been so loud?*

It's hard not to ask those *what if* questions. But when we focus on the *what ifs*, we forget the wins. And for us, there *were* wins. We hosted two sold-out farm-to-table dinners that raised over $100,000 for our community. We weren't able to use those dollars to save the building like we originally intended. But they will go a long way in bringing other economic development opportunities and revival efforts to our town.

There are yet more buildings to save, new dreams to build, other victories to claim. I hope you see that even when a dream falters, the effort isn't wasted. We've scored some big wins, and now we adjust our vision and keeping moving forward.

What's the best that could happen?

WHEN THE ROSE-COLORED GLASSES COME OFF

Because we're dreamers, it's easy to approach this journey with rose-colored glasses. We're willing to look fear in the eye and say, "I'm going for it," because our passion outranks the risk.

Many of these dreams have been stirring in our hearts for years, and once we finally take the leap to pursue them, once we finally discover our purpose, we think, *Finally life will be easier and more fulfilling.* But as the classic John Conlee song goes:

These rose-colored glasses
That I'm looking through
Show only the beauty
'Cause they hide all the truth.

When you get to this stage of the game, you'll find some good news and some bad news. The good news: Knowing your purpose brings clarity and a path forward. The bad news: Living out your purpose is still hard, just a different kind of hard.

I don't want you to be fooled into thinking your journey will be nothing but smooth sailing, because it rarely is. And when the rose-colored glasses come off, you might find yourself doubting that your dream is still real. You may think, *Is this really what God is asking me to do?*

When you feel unqualified and think maybe you've missed the mark, or when chasing the dream is harder than you ever imagined—this is where faith steps in. There's really no way to have faith without first having doubt. Because when you're confident you can do something, you don't require any faith. It's when you feel that you can't do something that your faith gets stirred and gives you the courage to keep going, even when the way forward is hard.

Think of someone you look up to as a hero, someone you admire for their great success. The thing is, being a hero and being successful is not an easy accomplishment. Heroes face battles, and battles require faith. But faith doesn't mean easy. A.W. Tozer once said, "We can be in our day what the heroes of faith were in their day—but remember, at the time they didn't know they were heroes."

You may not feel like a hero. And if this is the case, you're in good company! We tend to forget that heroes are *people* just like us. They didn't have all the answers. They just said yes to God's calling regardless of how impossible it seemed.

Maybe you feel that you don't have what it takes to do this thing stirring in your heart. Maybe you can't fathom that God wants to use you. But God has a way of taking people who don't view themselves as qualified and working through them in the most extraordinary ways. He has a way of pointing them out and saying, *You—yes you—I want to use you, I want to make you into who you never thought you could be. I want to change generations through your life.*

Hold onto the clarity of your purpose and let it be your guiding light.

What's the best that could happen?

YOU WERE BORN TO FLY

The power of small isn't about scale—it's about heart, grit, and the audacity to dream where others see limits. In rural America, small towns aren't just surviving; they're redefining what it means to thrive.

For years small towns have watched the exodus of talent to cities, but I think the secret's out: Small towns still have plenty of room for dreamers and doers to thrive.

You don't need a skyscraper to soar—just a community that's got your back. These are places where one idea can light up a whole town, where old buildings hold new promise, and where community pride turns potential into action. It's a vision that sees home not as a steppingstone, but as a destination.

Nothing stirs the soul like watching someone live out their calling in a small town. Because one person's dream can bring hope to an entire community, inspiring others to dare to ask, *What if I could, too?* That's the allure of rural America—one dream put into action can spark the transformation of a quiet town into a beacon of possibility.

Stay true to your story. Your authenticity is your strength—no one can chase your dream like you can. If God planted it in your heart, it's there for a purpose, a calling you're meant to chase with everything you've got. Dreams give you something to reach for, a reason to get up every morning, even when the path isn't clear. No matter how big they seem, never let anyone convince you they're out of reach.

You weren't meant to live out your days stuck in a small town, feeling like nothing's possible. You were born to chase your dreams and fly—right here. As Nicole Smith of *Dream Dirt* puts it, "If you don't just jump in and do it, there's never gonna be the perfect time. So just commit. And you align yourself with the people who are in what you want to do, and you grab your mentor, and you learn. And the more knowledge you build, the more confidence you have, and you just fly."

What's the best that could happen?

FIGHT FOR YOUR DREAM

I've lived the highs and lows of chasing dreams in rural America—moments that felt straight out of a movie and others that brought me to my knees. Our journey doesn't always go like we thought it would. We can have the best of hopes and run into the biggest disappointments we never dreamed were possible. But we keep going. Because nothing worthwhile in life comes easy. As Theodore Roosevelt said, "Nothing in the world is worth having or worth doing unless it means effort, pain, difficulty. I have never in my life envied a human being who led an easy life. I have envied a great many people who led difficult lives and led them well." It's through this grit and perseverance that true character is formed.

Oftentimes the high road is the hard road. It's the road we wish we didn't have to take. But I hope you'll take it anyway. I hope you'll continue to believe in your town for what it could be, instead of what it has been. I hope you'll find friends to lean on in the good times and the bad. I hope you'll choose to speak positivity when it feels like everyone around you speaks negativity. I hope you'll never quit believing that rural America is filled with opportunity. I hope you'll know you're exactly where you're supposed to be at this exact moment in time. And I hope you'll never stop dreaming, no matter what you're up against.

Without dreams, life feels stagnant. Communities stagnate too when people stop dreaming. Not surprising, because the Book of Proverbs tells us that where there is no vision, people will perish. Interestingly, another word for perish is *decay*. Every person has a role to play to make the community thrive. Imagine if everyone in your town pursued their purpose—what a vibrant place it would be. Your dream may be the very thing to spark that change, inspiring others to follow.

Once you get clarity on your dream, hang onto it with all you've got and—whatever you do—do not give up. Kevin Costner once said, "I think people throw away their dreams too early. Especially in this country. You have to have a car, you have to get a house, and you have to get a lot of things. And I think, in America, dreams are the first things to go for people. They get out of college, their life starts, and they throw their dreams away. And I think dreams should be the last things to go in our lives."

Don't throw away your dream. Those whispers of doubt—*It's too late. I'm not enough. This town's too small. I don't feel supported.*—are lies meant to keep you from the greatness you're made for. You're not here by chance. God placed you in your rural corner of the world, at this exact moment, to shine.

So, what if you dare to chase your dream? Not only could it change your life, but it could change your community and the lives of the people around you. And as others watch you step out and pursue your dream, it gives them the courage to think, *Maybe I could do that too.*

Perhaps you're thinking, *Who am I to do this? Who am I to make a difference in my community?* I'm here to tell you that you're exactly the right person to do this.

What will people say? I'll be honest. Some may say, "That'll never work" and give some sad eyes when you step out and go for it. Don't listen to them! Trust your heart. Trust the dream God placed in you. Fight for it. It's bigger than you think, and it's not just for you—others need you to live it.

What's the best that can happen?

LET'S GO CHANGE THE WORLD

Stepping out of your comfort zone takes faith. It takes grit. But honestly, if your dream doesn't scare you, it's probably not big enough. Whatever God is calling you to, I hope you'll say yes. I promise you, God is not done writing your story.

Anything worth doing is going to be hard. It will bring the highest of highs and lowest of lows. But every rejection, every breakdown, every sleepless night is a brick in the foundation of this dream. And every twist, turn, hill, and valley just might be worth it to pursue what's in your heart.

You—yes, you—are called to change the world. We all are. But there are only a few who will truly step out and be world changers. Who will accept the call and live out the fullness of what God has for his or her life? Will that be you? I pray it is. Rural America needs exactly what you have, and you're the only person with your exact gifting and talents and calling who can bring it to the world. Will you answer the call?

What's the best that can happen?

★

ACTIVATION

What dream feels impossible because you haven't explored it or given it a name?

What negative situation do you need to flip to a positive turning point in your life?

What's the best that can happen if you were to chase your dream?

CHAPTER ELEVEN

FLIP THE SCRIPT AND FORGE THE FUTURE

★

"The future belongs to those who believe in the beauty of their dreams."
— *Eleanor Roosevelt*

For years, our small towns weathered a drought—a drought of hope. Main Streets grew quiet and dreams seemed to wither under the weight of "what's always been." But now, I feel it—a shift in the air, like the fresh scent of rain rolling in from the horizon. Not fear, but hope. Change. Courage. A downpour of possibility ready to break over rural America.

Our towns are ripe with potential, bursting with opportunity. The question isn't whether the future can be bright—it's whether we'll step into our purpose to seize it. Revival won't come easy. It'll take hard work, years of perseverance, and hearts brave enough to dream where others see limits. But imagine rural America not as a place of limits, but as a field of dreams, where one bold idea can ripple out and change everything. That world isn't just possible—it's waiting for you to build it.

So how do you forge a path forward that makes the most of these opportunities?

FLIP THE SCRIPT

For too long, rural America has been cast as a fading backdrop—towns drying up, talent fleeing to cities, Main Streets crumbling into disrepair. But that's the old script, and it's time to tear it up. Rural America isn't a place of limits; it's a powerhouse of opportunity, where dreamers build thriving communities with grit and heart.

To flip the script is to rewrite this story, to show the world that small towns are where innovation, belonging, and possibility collide. The flip is about turning your town into a field of dreams, where one bold move draws others to build alongside you.

So, what would it look like if we actually flipped the script on rural America? What could this look like for your town? The answer lies in these four fundamental steps.

Step one: Start by redefining your town as a destination, not a departure point. It's time to move beyond the tired idea that success means leaving for the bright city lights. Small towns are where the dreamers stay and shine, like *Diamond Cross Ranch* in Moran, Wyoming, where the Gollihers, whose story appears in chapter 5, overcame impossible odds to save a ranch and continue a legacy. Highlight these stories—on social media, in local papers, or through platforms like *Rural Revival*—to show that big dreams thrive here. Market the quality of life that cities can't touch, including wide-open spaces, neighbors who know your name, and a pace that lets you breathe. As Sheri Glazier of *Dirt Road Dietician* puts it, "Rural America is community, and that's what everybody's seeking right now."

Invite young people back and newcomers in. Show them a place to plant roots and soar.

Step two: Turn the economic tide inward. The old narrative says corporate giants drain rural dollars, but you have the power to reverse that flow. Take a cue from Michael Stepp and Matt Dennis, whose online *Handlebend* copper brand pulls revenue from across the U.S. to small town Nebraska, creating local jobs and breathing new life into their downtown. Encourage entrepreneurs to leverage e-commerce to sell farm goods, crafts, or niche products not just locally but globally—and then reinvest those dollars into your town. Create entrepreneurial incubators or shared workspaces to cultivate startups such as coffee roasters or small manufacturers that can scale beyond local markets. Rally residents to support businesses that generate new wealth, not merely recycle the same local dollars. This isn't just business; it's a strategy to position your town as a hub for economic growth and prosperity.

Step three: Empower your dreamers to stay and build. The old script says the best and brightest must leave, but small towns are ripe for visionaries like Josh Smith of *Montana Knife Company*, who turned a twenty-year dream into a thriving reality without leaving home. Open up vacant storefronts, farmsteads, or community roles to young people eager to return or start fresh. Sell old buildings at a reasonable price that makes it possible for a business to start and succeed. Offer mentorship, low-cost leases, or community grants to help launch new businesses. Host vision-casting events to spark a culture of "what if," similar to the *What Could Be Tour* in Sumner, Iowa. This tour transformed vacant historic buildings into staged storefronts that showcased "what could be." When you back local talent, you not only keep people in your town—you help to fuel a revival that echoes for generations.

Step four: Lead with relentless vision and optimism. The old script thrives on complaints of empty buildings, tight budgets, and "we've tried that before," to name a few. Flip that script by becoming the voice of what's possible. Celebrate every win, from a new shop to a school fundraiser, and build momentum with tangible steps. Create a *yes culture* that sparks new businesses and events. Find mentors—mayors, business owners, or community leaders—who've driven change and empower others to join your vision. As Dan Douglas of *Belleville Hometown Lumber* says, "Do I want to play a part in our community's growth? Absolutely, one hundred percent." You can be the leader who ignores the skeptics, shows others what's possible, and turns your town into a beacon of hope.

"Flip the script" isn't a cute slogan—it's a call to action. Your town isn't a thing of the past. It's a gift to a world that craves connection, purpose, and belonging. Start today. You're not called to merely rewrite a narrative—you're called to forge a future where rural America leads the way.

LEAD WITH VISION

Great leaders don't just talk—they act. They paint a clear picture of what's possible and rally others to make it happen, especially in small towns where change can be an uphill battle. Leadership here isn't about grand gestures. It's about starting something real and inspiring others to join in. For me and my town, it began with a mural—a small step that sparked hope.

One fall, I found myself with a few free days before harvest kicked into full gear and I was needed to drive the grain cart. I noticed a blank wall on a building along our town's main highway, and it got my creative wheels spinning. The building was weathered and plain, but I couldn't shake the thought: *What if we painted a mural here?* A splash of color, something to make a good impression of our town as people passed through. I pitched the idea to the local ag business who owned the building, and they were immediately on board. So, I grabbed some paint and got to work.

I didn't expect much—it was just a small gesture to make our town feel alive. But something unexpected happened. Neighbors sent cards and handwritten notes, saying, "Thank you for believing in our town." That mural was more than just paint on a wall—it was a sign that our community could be more. It got people to ask, *What's next?* One simple act ignited ideas, excitement, and dreams I didn't know our town was holding.

Leadership in a small town means starting that momentum and keeping it alive. It's not about having all the answers or doing it alone. It's about showing others what's possible and empowering them to join in. Here are some ways to lead with vision and purpose in your community:

- **Cast vision relentlessly.** Oftentimes you must change mindsets that have been in place for decades in your community, and this shift doesn't happen overnight. Continue to cast vision and paint a picture of what could be—a place where Main Street thrives, opportunities and experiences flourish, and people are proud to call it home. Change takes time, but the more you show people what's possible, the more they will buy in.

- **Build momentum.** One win—whether a mural, a fundraiser, or a new shop opening—can kick things off. Build on that first win with steady, practical steps. Momentum is hard to start, especially when people

173

grumble or progress seems slow. But once things get moving, that momentum snowballs. People get excited, ideas multiply, and suddenly, your town is alive with dreamers chasing their own visions.

- **Focus on the positive.** It's easy to criticize and pick apart what's wrong in your town. But great leaders focus on what's right and make it better. Be a cheerleader and celebrate the wins, no matter how small. Talk up the new business opening, the volunteer cleanup crew, the kid who started a community garden. Your positivity is contagious —it shifts the conversation from "we can't" to "we will"— and pulls people together.

- **Find mentors.** No leader goes it alone. I lean on mayors and leaders who've been in the trenches because their wisdom sharpens my own. Find mentors who inspire you, who have seen revival take hold, and ask for their guidance. They'll help you navigate challenges to become the leader your town needs.

- **Empower others.** The greatest leaders empower people. They cast a vision and inspire others to step up and bring their own skills and talents to the table. Encourage their ideas, support their dreams, and give them room to shine. When you empower people, you're not just fixing a problem—you're building a team that can transform your town.

Leadership isn't about being the loudest or the most powerful. It's about believing in your town when others don't, taking steps forward, and showing others they can do it too. It's about painting a mural when no one asked for it, about sparking hope that inspires others to dream.

Be the leader who says yes to the vision, who defies the naysayers, who shows your town what it can become. Your action can start a chain reaction that changes your town for good. Revival begins when more people catch the vision and make it their own.

RAISED TO STAY

A few years back, at an FFA conference for high school girls in Iowa, I led a table discussion that changed my perspective. After completing my planned question-and-answer session with the first group ahead of schedule, I asked a spontaneous question. "If the right jobs and opportunities were here, how many of you would stay in or return to your small town after college?" Every hand shot up. I was stunned. I knew some young people wanted to stay in their small towns, but I hadn't realized the desire was so strong.

I asked the same question to group after group at my table that day. Out of hundreds of girls, only a handful said they'd leave—and only because their dreams demanded it. That moment lit a fire in me. These young women *wanted* to stay. What if we could make this possible? What if our towns became places where the next generation could thrive?

That question isn't just meant for our kids—it's meant for all of us who have the power to flip the script in our small towns.

Do most young people in your town feel they have to leave after graduation? What would it take to make your community a vibrant place to build a life? Success doesn't have to mean leaving. It's on us—as parents, leaders, neighbors—to create opportunities that give our kids a real choice to stay. Mike

McCartney, executive director of the *Pawhuska Chamber of Commerce*, captures what's at stake. "When you keep your eye on the prize and your baby girl moves home, that means something." Whether it's jobs, mentorship, opportunities to open a coffee shop, a gym, or a path to take over a retiring business, we can shape a future where staying feels like a dream worth chasing.

This is why I launched *Raised to Stay*, a movement to transform rural America by fostering opportunities and shifting mindsets. It's about spotting the gaps—retiring business owners whose shops could be passed on, unmet needs for new ventures, or missing pieces such as community events that spark connection. Libby Timmerman, who renovated two historic buildings in her town, shows how it's done. "Keeping kids involved is key. I bring my high school girls to the studio, showing them what's possible." Dakota Dawn Johnson sees it too. "There's a bigger perspective of what's possible in rural America. I want to raise good humans who contribute to it." Their efforts prove that an investment in the next generation keeps our towns alive.

If you're a student, speak up—tell your community what you need to stay or return. Your voice matters. If you're a leader, listen and act. As Kevin Cabbage reflects, "There's nothing like returning home, but what am I returning to?" Let's rewrite the story of rural America. Let's build towns where our kids choose to stay, where dreams take root, and communities thrive for generations. Join the *Raised to Stay* movement at ruralrevival.co/raisedtostay and help shape that future.

MAKE SPACE FOR THE NEXT GENERATION

Our rural landscape was forged by dreamers—pioneers who settled these lands with bold visions, not just to make a living but to leave a legacy for future generations. Today, rural America is *our* new frontier, brimming with potential. But for it to thrive, we must make room for those who follow behind us. Young people, many who grew up here, are eager to return and breathe fresh life into our Main Streets, farms, and communities. But if there's no place for them to live, no one willing to pass the torch, the small-town dream will slip out of their reach.

My challenge to rural America is this: Make a space for the next generation. Welcome them. Believe in their vision. Cheer them on. Entrust young dreamers with vacant buildings, family acreages, and opportunities to build. Their dreams may look different from those of past generations, but what if your town became place where new families could build their own legacies?

Shanda Mattix, owner of *Barnwood & Bling* boutique and *Prairie Barn Market* in Colby, Kansas, roots her purpose in making space for the next generation. "So much of what we do, we're doing to serve a need that is in our community," Shanda says. "Because ultimately we want this place to be a place that all generations feel welcomed and involved and there's things for them to do and participate in, a place that our kids and our friends' kids and our family are able to thrive."

New Providence, Iowa is thriving because they made space for the next generation. Oftentimes people want to put high price tags on old historic buildings that haven't been kept up for decades. In New Providence, where six millennial entrepreneurs chose to start businesses in a population of 250, the locals who offered reasonable prices on these historic buildings made it possible to bring these businesses to life here. The young business owners credit this factor as a significant part of their success and their ability to run a profitable business. They've also seen the community rally around and support them every chance they get.

Stanton, Iowa has experienced a similar revival, where Kevin Cabbage and *FMTC*, the local telephone cooperative, partnered with the city to hire Jenna Ramsey as a community development director. This partnership has allowed the community to receive over $5 million in grants in five years—and their Main Street is thriving because of it. Restored facades, new businesses growth, and a future full of possibility are a product of Stanton's people and partners working together.

Imagine the impact—vibrant communities, transformed by fresh energy and ideas—all because we dared to make space. A future where our towns not only survive but thrive, where our populations start growing instead of shrinking. We're stewards of both our history and our future. We have the opportunity to transform the places that held our ancestors' dreams into vital communities where the next generation can soar. Will you help build this future?

A DELICATE BALANCE

Since I launched *Rural Revival*, I've seen the rural landscape shift. I attribute this shift to the remarkable revival efforts of many people, improved internet connectivity, more remote job opportunities, and a post-COVID change in perspective. It's a welcome change, and as a result, people are seeking rural life more than ever before, drawn by simplicity, escape, and the promise of a better life. If ever there was a time for rural America to shine, this is it.

But as we embrace this opportunity, we must protect what makes these places special. The authentic, endearing heart of rural communities is what pulls people in. It's a delicate balance between welcoming progress while remaining true to our roots.

I've witnessed many rural places undergo remarkable transformations in ways that honor their past while building a vibrant future that fits the local culture. Sadly, I've also seen examples where this hasn't been the case. I've seen newcomers, captivated by small town charm, arrive with plans to reshape these communities. But then, they ultimately turn them into the very places they came from—the places they hoped to escape.

Whether you're new to rural America or you are returning after years away, your vision and ambition are likely a breath of fresh air. But as you start to chase your dreams here, it's important that you tread lightly. Before you push for change, take time to listen and learn. Discover the things that make this place special. Immerse yourself in the culture. Find out what sets this community apart. Learn which projects are already in the works. You might be surprised by what you find here—things you didn't see when you were just visiting for an occasional weekend.

When I moved back to my hometown, I started by observing —how things worked, what initiatives were already going on, and where the gaps were—the projects and needs that nobody else was working on. Different groups around town asked me to share my vision for the community, which I enjoyed doing. But I didn't act until I identified a need that no one else was meeting. For my town, that need was to revive our Main Street, bring in new businesses, and save historic buildings from demolition.

Find the unique gap in your community and focus your efforts there. Honor your town's culture and history and tie it to your vision. You'll find your place to make a difference. But make sure you don't change too much of what makes this place special.

Progress should amplify, not overwrite, the soul of rural America—its history, its people, its heart. Let's revive our towns while staying true to the reasons we call them home. Because this is the cornerstone of this life we've chosen—the solid foundation upon which we build.

FORGE A FUTURE TOGETHER

Rural America stands at a crossroads. The drought of hope is breaking, and a downpour of possibility is on the way. But forging the future means that all of us—newcomers, lifelong residents, young dreamers—must work together. It means working to balance progress with preservation, making space for the next generation, and acting with courage when the moment calls. It means flipping the script, embracing our strengths, and leading with vision that inspires.

You are the heart of this revival. Your dream, your grit, your faith can transform your town into a field of dreams where others come to build too. As Michael Stepp says, "We're promoting slowing down, spending time with people, unplugging from the rat race." These are the best parts of rural America—a place where community is the currency, where quality of life slows you down and fills you up, where one big idea can change everything. This is where small town dreamers thrive—*and you're right in the center of it.*

On those days when you may feel like you're all your town has, know this: you are all it needs. That fire in your heart is there for a reason. You were chosen to carry this vision. You were meant to lead, to inspire, to shape the future of your community. Don't waver. Keep going. You've got more in you than you know. The vision is bigger than you, but it begins with you. This is your moment, and our small towns need your courage.

Imagine your town a hundred years from now—alive with possibility, thriving because of the seeds you plant today. The future of rural America is not just a hope, it's built on the big dreams and resilient spirit you invest in your community now.

So step boldly into your calling. Chase your dream with arms wide open. Be the spark that lights the fire. Go write a story that will echo through the ages—full of grit, grace, and a whole lot of heart—and give it everything you've got. For in your dreams lies the heartbeat of rural America, and with every step, you bring it to life.

Join the *Raised to Stay* movement at ruralrevival.co/raisedtostay and help shape the future for the next generation.

Want to get people dreaming about "what could be" in your small town? Our What Could Be Tour Kit has everything you need to put on a tour in your town— including guides, templates, and tips to set you up for success and provide a great experience for your community! Get the kit at ruralrevival.co/whatcouldbetour.

★

ACTIVATION

What's one small step you can take to spark excitement and community pride in your town?

What's a mindset in your community that people rarely challenge, like "That's how it's always been"? How can you share a vision to shift that perspective toward possibility?

Think of a recent win in your town, no matter how small. How can you use that win to build momentum and get others excited about what's possible?

What positive things are already happening in your community that you can cheer on?

Who could serve as a mentor to guide your leadership efforts—a local leader, mayor, or business owner who's driven change? What steps will you take to connect and learn from them?

How can you invite others into your vision for your town?

What do you want your small town to look like in one hundred years?

How can you encourage the next generation to see rural America as a place of opportunity rather than a place to leave? What can you do to create opportunities for them?

If you're part of the next generation, what would it take for you to stay?

CLOSING

Ever since I started this *Rural Revival* journey, I knew deep in my heart I found what I was created to do. God called me to it, and as crazy as it was to jump in with *no* idea how it would go, it just felt right. Seven years later, I can say with unwavering confidence that there's nothing more fulfilling than walking in His divine plan. As always, thanks for being one of the most important pieces of this dream.

I hope and pray whenever you listen to the podcast, join one of our events, or read these pages, I can be a bright spot in your day—that our conversations and content can uplift and encourage you. Thank you from the bottom of my heart for following along.

My goal is to provide resources that empower you to thrive in your small business and small town. Please visit ruralrevival.co and follow us on social media to join our *Rural Revival* community as we chase our dreams together. I would love for you to tag or email me as you set out on this journey so I can encourage and cheer you on!

Danna Larson

ABOUT THE AUTHOR

Danna Larson, the dynamic voice and visionary behind *Rural Revival*, ignites inspiration for small-town dreamers through her podcast, platform, and speaking engagements. As founder and host, she champions the entrepreneurs revitalizing rural communities with passion and purpose.

Danna is a graduate of Iowa State University with a B.A. in Public Relations, and her career spans roles as a corporate advertising account executive, nonprofit director of communications, and brand manager.

Now a seasoned entrepreneur, Danna empowers businesses to shine through her brand management firm, *Spark Seven*, and rural-focused design studio, *Branded by Rural Revival*. She is a skilled creator of moments that move people, helping clients amplify their messages and build brands that resonate deeply with audiences.

After years in the city, Danna has returned to her Iowa farm roots, driven by a mission to rekindle the spirit of rural America. Having traveled rural America extensively, she's inspired by its resilience and untapped potential.

When she's not working on the farm, growing her businesses, or dreaming up her next big idea, you'll find Danna cruising back roads, soaking in the music and stories of rural life—drawing inspiration to help others to flourish in their businesses and communities.

BOOK DANNA AS A SPEAKER

Interested in having Danna join you as a keynote or breakout speaker? No matter the event, Danna speaks and teaches on topics that empower and inspire people to build momentum and thrive in their business and community. Visit ruralrevival.co/founder and let's talk more!

BRANDED BY RURAL REVIVAL

We're a rural-focused design studio empowering small businesses and towns to build brands they love. From websites and brand design to logos and podcasting, our small-town team delivers authentic, impactful designs, including customizable website templates, to help your vision thrive. Find more at brandedbyruralrevival.co.

FIND RURAL REVIVAL ONLINE

ruralrevival.co
smalltowndreamer.co
instagram.com/ruralrevivalco
facebook.com/ruralrevivalco
youtube.com/ruralrevivalco

RESOURCES

RURAL REVIVAL PODCAST

Rural Revival is a captivating podcast hosted by Danna Larson, celebrating the heart and hustle of small-town entrepreneurs revitalizing rural America. Through inspiring stories, practical insights, and a passion for community, Danna spotlights the dreamers and doers breathing new life into rural landscapes. Tune in to discover the resilience, creativity, and potential of small-town life!

MADE RURAL

Made Rural is a new podcast and platform hosted by Danna Larson, empowering you to break free from limitations, discover your divine calling, and impact the world around you. With uplifting guest speakers, actionable wisdom, and heartfelt encouragement, Danna champions your journey as you chase big dreams in small places. Your purpose awaits—this is your time to shine!

FARM DINNER EVENT KIT

Want to host a farm-to-table dinner of your own? Our Farm Dinner Event Kit covers every part of your planning—from organizing volunteers to ticket sales to creating an unforgettable experience for everyone involved, plus tips and tricks we've learned along the way. Get the kit at ruralrevival.co/farmdinner.

WHAT COULD BE TOUR KIT

Want to get people dreaming about "what could be" in your small town? Our What Could Be Tour Kit has everything you need to put on a tour in your town—including guides, templates, and tips to set you up for success and provide a great experience for your community! Get the kit at ruralrevival.co/whatcouldbetour.

RAISED TO STAY

Join the *Raised to Stay* movement at ruralrevival.co/raisedtostay and help shape the future for the next generation.

DARE TO DREAM SESSIONS

Ready to explore those dreams in your heart? If you know there's more to life than what you're currently experiencing, book a Dare to Dream session and let's help you discover your divine purpose and calling!

VISIONING WORKSHOPS

Reviving a town doesn't happen overnight, but a great plan and an inspired group of leaders can take you a lot farther, a lot faster. Let's create a plan to help you move forward!

STRATEGIC CONSULTING

Often the success of your business or town comes down to an effective strategy—one that puts your vision and goals into motion. Let's create a plan to help you move forward!